IMAGES
of America

HOLLYWOOD ON THE POTOMAC

To Connie —
This STAR of JCS!
Enjoy!

[signature]

STATE, WAR, AND NAVY BUILDING, WASHINGTON, D.C., APRIL 1918. Silent movie actor Charlie Chaplin became one of the first screen actors to jump into the political arena, delivering a pitch to raise money for the Third Liberty Loan benefiting U.S. forces in World War I. Film stars were a brand-new phenomenon and were already wielding off-screen influence. This is believed to be one of the first photographs to show a major star jumping into the fray of politics. (Courtesy National Archives.)

ON THE COVER: Pres. John F. Kennedy sails with actor, and brother-in-law, Peter Lawford aboard the U.S. Coast Guard yacht *Manitou* off the coast of Maine in August 1962. When Kennedy's sister Patricia married Lawford, it was one of the first marriages of politics and Hollywood. Lawford was a member of the Rat Pack, a famous entertainment line-up that included Frank Sinatra, Dean Martin, Sammy Davis Jr., and Joey Bishop. The group of superstars often campaigned for Kennedy, prompting Sinatra to give Kennedy the nickname "Brother-in-Lawford." (Courtesy Robert Knudsen, White House/John F. Kennedy Presidential Library, Boston.)

IMAGES
of America

HOLLYWOOD ON THE POTOMAC

Jason Killian Meath

ARCADIA
PUBLISHING

Copyright © 2009 by Jason Killian Meath
ISBN 978-0-7385-6755-6

Published by Arcadia Publishing
Charleston SC, Chicago IL, Portsmouth NH, San Francisco CA

Printed in the United States of America

Library of Congress Control Number: 2008943870

For all general information contact Arcadia Publishing at:
Telephone 843-853-2070
Fax 843-853-0044
E-mail sales@arcadiapublishing.com
For customer service and orders:
Toll-Free 1-888-313-2665

Visit us on the Internet at www.arcadiapublishing.com

For Renee and Aidan

CONTENTS

ACKNOWLEDGMENTS

The research and writing of this book would never have been possible without the generous support of many individuals and institutions: Maggie Bullwinkel, Brooksi Hudson, and everyone else at Arcadia Publishing; Amy Marino (Williams Mullen); Mary Finch (George Bush Presidential Library); Kimberlee Lico (Ronald Reagan Presidential Library); Christina Rodriguez (LBJ Library); Polly Nodine (Jimmy Carter Library); Maryrose Grossman (John Fitzgerald Kennedy Library); Nancy Mirshah (Gerald Ford Presidential Library); Darla Thompson (Eisenhower Presidential Library); John Keller (William J. Clinton Presidential Library); Ed Gillespie; Amy Zantzinger; Jeanie Mamo and Julie Cram (the White House, George W. Bush Administration); Pete Souza and Sandra Eisert (the White House, Barack Obama Administration); Stuart Stevens and Russ Schriefer (the Stevens and Schriefer Group); Heather Moore (Senate Historical Office); Buddy Bynum (Office of Gov. Haley Barbour); Mark Hayes (Office of Sen. Richard G. Lugar); Mark McKinnon; Don Mischer (Don Mischer Productions); Dan Glickman (Motion Picture Association of America); Robin Bronk (the Creative Coalition); David Fuscus (Xenophon Strategies); Rhoda Glickman; Jonathan Shapiro; Steve Cohen; Neil Godsey; David Landis; Joe Crimmings; and as always, Mom and Dad.

INTRODUCTION

When Frank Capra unveiled *Mr. Smith Goes to Washington*, he introduced a young, idealistic Jimmy Stewart punching his congressional card, ready to right the country back on its axis. But when the film was released in 1939, it was bitterly denounced by old-time Washington insiders and panned by the establishment press—hardly surprising. The D.C. insider crowd forgot to gauge America's pulse, and *Mr. Smith Goes to Washington* went on to become a national treasure.

When Hollywood jumps into politics, it can be an awkward pairing—like a first date—filled with pitfalls, crags in the road, and bizarre photo ops that often amount to little else than paparazzo fodder. But to discount the earnest determination by America's celebrity culture to play politics would be a mistake. Something deeper is at work. Hollywood, at heart, is filled with dreamers of grand things, whether rooted in fairy tale or fact. Politicos are big dreamers, too, but they must also be pragmatists. When Hollywood comes to town, it can be the perfect foil for Washington's stoic, often cynical, culture.

The nation is often unsure what to make of it when Hollywood plays politics—a *CBS News* poll from 2007 found that 47 percent believed Hollywood stars could offer useful fresh perspectives on political issues while 48 percent said they should keep out of politics. There is no doubt that the role stars have played in American politics has changed over time.

The nation's "War Stars" during World War II—Rita Hayworth, Bing Crosby, and Danny Kaye, among many others—solidified Hollywood's official role in America's national agenda. The most talked-about roles for entertainers were not on screen but in front of war-torn troops, boosting morale on the front lines and leading the charge on the home front.

That kind of wartime support from Hollywood may have faded, but it never died. Stars like Bruce Willis, Toby Keith, and Gary Sinise carried the torch to the Middle East and tirelessly gave back during the post-9/11 wars of Iraq and Afghanistan. But there can be little doubt: Hollywood—like the rest of the country—was never as unified as it was during World War II. Through civil rights, Vietnam, and Iraq, Hollywood stars became as divided and diverse in political opinions as everyone else, and were often accused of leaning decidedly to the left.

John Wayne was an unabashed conservative, and Jane Fonda was an outspoken liberal. But historically speaking, most big-name stars fall somewhere in the middle—Frank Sinatra, Sammy Davis Jr., Kirk Douglas, Johnny Cash, and many others supported both Republicans and Democrats. Moreover, more and more stars in the decades that followed World War II began to adopt pet causes of all stripes, and just like passing a bill in Congress, they had to get along with all sides in order to see real progress.

It can be a perilous path for someone more accustomed to walking the red carpet than getting examined under the microscope of politics. Let's face it; many celebrities are fabulously rich, and no one wants to hear a sermon coming from a millionaire. Big stars pleading for the downtrodden or curbs on greenhouse gases have often fallen into the trap of chartering their own fossil fuel–belching private planes from L.A. to D.C.—earning the reputation as "limousine liberals" or even "gulfstream liberals."

"Celebrities are not looking for personal publicity," says NBC writer/producer Jonathan Shapiro (*Boston Legal, The Practice*). "They are naïve sometimes, but they really believe they can make a difference."

Celebrities champion diverse causes. They stump for issues that affect them personally or touch their heart—human rights, breast cancer, child poverty—name a hotspot anywhere in the world and there is likely an actor or rock star who is ready to stand up and fight. They can be the perfect mouthpiece that moves a nation toward compassion and understanding or to their checkbooks. Given their extraordinary gift of showmanship, and the often dry world of political advocacy, famous entertainers can become masterful messengers.

Big-name personalities cannot seem to help themselves when it comes to political opinions—they are Americans and they are entitled. And politicians are usually saps when famous faces come knocking on the door. "Almost everyone in Hollywood wants to be in politics and everyone in Washington wants to be in pictures," says political advisor and communications guru Mark McKinnon. While it may seem at times like an awkward first date, it endures as a spicy love affair between power and personality, pomp and pageantry.

The hundreds of snapshots presented here tell an evolutionary tale of our increasingly celebrity culture and its influence on American politics. This book offers many rare photographs of places and events that are sometimes forgotten but nonetheless important moments in history. It is far from being a complete anthology—the Hollywood blacklist, many notorious protests, and even a chronology of star-packed state dinners would fill a multi-volume set.

Rather, this book tells the human story of very famous and successful people who never stopped being Americans. Just the same, it is a rarely explored glimpse into our nation's leaders—all of whom embraced stardom at some level and incorporated its appeal into public life.

There is no single reason or lone cause that pigeonholes Hollywood and Washington's relationship. Different celebrities visit different politicians for a whole variety of reasons: sometimes for policy, sometimes for play—or sometimes they just happened to be in the neighborhood.

Scouring 11 different presidential libraries, the U.S. Capitol, National Archives, and more, this book presents a retrospective of the Hollywood-Washington relationship in five acts. Now let the drama unfurl and fireworks fly when Hollywood lands on the Potomac.

One

GALAS AND GLITTERATI

"There's no mix like a mix at the White House!" exclaims Hollywood producer Don Mischer—and he should know. The Emmy-award-winning producer crafted Washington spectacles from the Kennedy Center Honors to political conventions and presidential inaugurations. Mischer has witnessed for decades that "Hollywood and Washington are just so impressed with one another." And at first glance, the pictures jolt the imagination—the president and a supermodel confab at the Kennedy Center. . . . The First Lady dances with a crooner in the East Room. . . . Something electrifying is in the air. This is star power at the highest wattage. The White House, as with many of the public buildings in Washington, leads a double life: a serious place of work but also a grand backdrop for some of the world's most sought-after parties. As television brought entertainers, sports heroes, and politicians into American living rooms, it gave all of them a new reason to appear together, unifying the best and brightest in the nation before the eyes of the world. Harry Truman's inauguration ceremony became the first to be televised. Perhaps not coincidentally, Truman reinstated the tradition of inaugural balls, bringing together famous names and faces to lift America's spirits after World War II. The Kennedys spun the Camelot mystique, summoning the most glittering stars to dazzling parties, and Washington suddenly became fashionable again. There is something about politicians—whether liberal or conservative—that makes them remarkably at ease among the biggest celebrities. What makes Bill Clinton, from small-town Hope, Arkansas, so comfortable around the biggest names and egos in the world? "Clinton was star struck," says Steven Cohen, who spent eight years with President Clinton in the White House. Cohen, who is now is creative director of Michael Eisner's Tornante Company, observes that "it doesn't matter how many Academy Awards or Super Bowl rings anyone has, the oval office levels the playing field." But if there were big stars and rollicking entertainment, Clinton capitalized on it. "He was more game to have fun with things," says Mischer. "Clinton would sing along, cry when things on stage were sad—he would react so dramatically. And, he was keenly aware when the camera was on him." The fact is that celebrities and politicians are just happy to be part of the show. If the presidency is the biggest role you can ever play, the White House is the world's perfect stage.

NBC Studios, Burbank, California, December 1985. Pres. Ronald Reagan and First Lady Nancy Reagan attend television's *All Star Tribute to Dutch Reagan*. Guests included, from left to right, (seated) Colleen Reagan, Neil Reagan, Maureen Reagan, the president, Nancy Reagan, and Ronald and Nancy's son-in-law Dennis Revell; (standing) entertainers Emmanuel Lewis, Charlton Heston, Ben Vereen, Monty Hall, Frank Sinatra, Burt Reynolds, Dean Martin, Eydie Gorme, Vin Scully, Steve Lawrence, and two unidentified. As a screen actor, Hollywood prepared Reagan for the political stage and gave him the knack to please his audience. During a speech to the entertainment industry crowd, he said, "When I first started in my present job, I'd sometimes put together in my mind my own dream Cabinet—you know, John Wayne as Secretary of State, Clint Eastwood at Defense, Jack Benny as Secretary of Treasury, Grouch Marx at Education." (Courtesy Ronald Reagan Library.)

WASHINGTON CONVENTION CENTER, WASHINGTON, D.C., JANUARY 1993. Pres. Bill Clinton jams with the band during the Arkansas Inaugural Ball. Clinton blurred lines between pop culture and politics like never before. The new president enlisted Hollywood producer Harry Thomason to produce a star-studded inaugural. Clinton wasn't just an onlooker; he was often part of the entertainment. (Courtesy William J. Clinton Presidential Library.)

PLAYHOUSE THEATER, WASHINGTON, D.C., MARCH 1956. Pres. Dwight Eisenhower is pictured at a premier of *Richard III* with Sir Laurence Olivier. From left to right are Mrs. Gordon Moore (Mamie Eisenhower's sister), Maj. John Eisenhower, British ambassador Sir Roger Makins, Olivier, First Lady Mamie Eisenhower, President Eisenhower, Elivera Doud (Mamie Eisenhower's mother), and unidentified. Olivier marked a historic event in American television. His film was simultaneously run in U.S. theaters and broadcast on NBC. Eisenhower was keenly aware of the changes television brought to American society. His 1956 reelection has been called the first television campaign. (Courtesy National Park Service, Dwight D. Eisenhower Presidential Library.)

PRIVATE RESIDENCE, NEW YORK, NEW YORK, MAY 1962. Pres. John F. Kennedy shares a laugh with Jimmy Durante. "Everybody wants to get inna de act," Durante famously said. With entertainers and Kennedy, it was true. Hollywood's biggest stars showed up at every opportunity to be seen with America's popular young president. (Courtesy Cecil Stoughton/John F. Kennedy Presidential Library, Boston.)

GRAND FOYER, THE WHITE HOUSE, JANUARY 1967. Pres. Lyndon Johnson dances with theatrical star Carol Channing after a performance of *Hello Dolly*. Channing often gave out her own awards she called "Diamond Awards"—actual diamond rings. Lady Bird Johnson was one recipient for her work beautifying America. As for President Johnson, he was an unabashed fan of Channing. It was speculated that this was a major reason Channing earned a spot on President Nixon's "Enemies List." (Photograph by Robert Knudsen; courtesy LBJ Library.)

ULINE ARENA, WASHINGTON, D.C., JANUARY 1946. Above, First Lady Bess Truman gives actor Cesar Romero a slice of cake during the Franklin D. Roosevelt Birthday Ball. Though FDR died a year earlier, Americans all over the nation participated in his birthday celebration because FDR always used the day to advance his most important cause—the fight to cure infantile paralysis. President Truman vowed to keep the tradition going and called upon the biggest stars to join him. Below, actor Van Johnson eats cake with actress Margaret O'Brien at the Birthday Ball. While packs of young girls swooned over Johnson, Hollywood's *Box Office* magazine cheekily reported, "The men whistled at [entertainers] Diana Lynn, Alexis Smith, Angela Lansbury and just hoped Margaret O'Brien would hurry up and be 18." (Both courtesy Harry S. Truman Library.)

GRAND FOYER, THE WHITE HOUSE, NOVEMBER 1985. Pres. Ronald Reagan entertained the royals of Great Britain by inviting American royalty from the big screen. For this gala dinner to honor the Prince of Wales and Princess Diana, guests included stars like Clint Eastwood, John Travolta, Tom Selleck, and singer Neil Diamond. Below, a radiant Princess Diana dances with actor and *Saturday Night Fever* star John Travolta. First Lady Nancy Reagan informed Travolta that the princess wanted a dance. What happened next electrified the crowd. At the time, Travolta's star power was lagging. But all the press frenzy over this dance put Travolta back on the map. In later interviews, he credited the infamous moment with revitalizing his film career. (Both courtesy Ronald Reagan Library.)

NATIONAL GUARD ARMORY, WASHINGTON, D.C., JANUARY 1949. Pres. Harry Truman poses with movie stars and others at his lavish inaugural ball, including, from left to right, actor Edgar Bergen, comedic actress Joan Davis, singer/actress Lena Horne, child actress Margaret O'Brien, actor George Jessel, four unidentified, Truman, actress/singer Alice Faye, actor Phil Regan, three unidentified, singer/dancer Jane Powell, unidentified, and actor Gene Kelly. For his inaugural, Truman was determined to put on a show. It was the most expensive and star-studded inauguration to date. It was also the first to be televised to the nation. (Courtesy Harry S. Truman Library.)

ENTRANCE HALL, THE WHITE HOUSE, FEBRUARY 1990. Pres. George H. W. Bush and First Lady Barbara Bush host a private dinner and screening of the movie *The Hunt for Red October* with actor James Earl Jones, among others. It is not surprising that the Bushes would make such a fuss over the patriotic cold war film. Jones played the role of director of the CIA in the film, which coincidentally was Bush's job from 1975 to 1977. (Courtesy George Bush Presidential Library.)

NATIONAL MALL, WASHINGTON, D.C., JANUARY 2009. Rock star Sting with his wife, Trudie Styler (center), and the Creative Coalition's Robin Bronk attend the 56th Presidential Inauguration. Pres. Barack Obama's inaugural was an all-day party as a crowd of over a million gathered to witness history. Many famous faces were among the throngs. Later Sting carried the party to the stage, joining Stevie Wonder to sing "Brand New Day." (Courtesy the Creative Coalition.)

GRAND FOYER, THE WHITE HOUSE, DECEMBER 1999. Pres. Bill Clinton greets Hollywood power couple Will Smith and Jada Pinkett Smith for America's Millennium Celebration. Will Smith was emcee for a gala at the Lincoln Memorial, one of many end-of-the-century bashes held around the world. As Smith performed hits from his latest rap album, he shouted out to Clinton to join the hundreds of thousands gathered on the National Mall and "Raise the roof, Bill." (Courtesy William J. Clinton Presidential Library.)

EAST ROOM, THE WHITE HOUSE, FEBRUARY 1981. Pres. Ronald Reagan attempts to "cut in" on First Lady Nancy Reagan and crooner Frank Sinatra's dance at the president's birthday party. Sinatra was a cherished family friend, and as a fellow performer, he and Nancy Reagan were known to break into song at official events. Sinatra even arranged Reagan's Presidential Gala, as he had for Pres. John F. Kennedy. (Courtesy Ronald Reagan Library.)

ULINE ARENA, WASHINGTON, D.C., JANUARY 1946. From left to right, Movie stars Angela Lansbury, Charles Coburn, and Constance Moore are seated at a table during a Franklin D. Roosevelt Birthday Ball. FDR died a year earlier, but his portrait, as his legacy, loomed over the background and the party. (Courtesy Harry S. Truman Library.)

PRIVATE RESIDENCE, NEW YORK, NEW YORK, MAY 1962. Pres. John F. Kennedy chats with comedian Jack Benny and Eunice Kennedy Shriver at Kennedy advisor Arthur Krim's party for the president's 45th birthday. Highly rated for 15 seasons, *The Jack Benny Show* was one of the longest running shows on television. Kennedy considered himself a loyal viewer—it was one of the only regular programs he made time to watch each week. (Courtesy Cecil Stoughton/John F. Kennedy Presidential Library, Boston.)

SHERATON PARK HOTEL, WASHINGTON, D.C., JUNE 1956. Pres. Dwight Eisenhower with, from left to right, entertainers Raymond Mouriks, Antonina Murio, Vic Damone, dancer/actress Jane Powell, Bob Hope, singer Pearl Bailey, and pianist Leonard Pennario are at the White House News Photographers Association's annual dinner. With the rise of television, mass media was becoming more and more influential. And Ike was catching on quick—catering to the media by flaunting a little star appeal at their annual dinner never hurts. (Courtesy National Park Service, Dwight D. Eisenhower Presidential Library.)

GROUND-FLOOR CORRIDOR, THE WHITE HOUSE, MARCH 1956. Film and television stars Roy Rogers and Dale Evans (wearing the hats) join Pres. Dwight Eisenhower for presidential grandson David's eighth birthday party. The singing cowboy and his wife were riding high with a hit television show, comics, and a whole set of action toys proudly displayed before the birthday boy. In fact, Rogers was second only to Walt Disney in merchandising to the kid crowd. And when a boy is the president's grandson, he doesn't just get the action figures—he gets the real-life stars to be the party entertainment. (Courtesy National Park Service, Dwight D. Eisenhower Presidential Library.)

SHERATON PARK HOTEL, WASHINGTON, D.C., APRIL 1962. Pres. John F. Kennedy is pictured at the White House Correspondents and News Photographers Dinner with, from left to right, unidentified, comic actor Peter Sellers, and British prime minister Harold Macmillan. Kennedy was a fan of Sellers. Years later, Sellers claimed his critically acclaimed, pallid portrayal of Pres. Merkin Muffley in *Dr. Strangelove* was modeled on Adlai Stevenson, whom Kennedy defeated for the Democratic nomination. (Courtesy Abbie Rowe, White House/John F. Kennedy Presidential Library, Boston.)

THE KENNEDY CENTER, WASHINGTON, D.C., JUNE 1977. Pres. Jimmy Carter, First Lady Rosalynn Carter, and daughter Amy pose with world-famous pantomime artist Marcel Marceau. Being a "first kid" comes with perks. After watching Marceau from the Presidential Box, the First Family met Marceau and his wife, Anne Sicco, backstage. Then the motorcade whisked the First Family back to the South Grounds of the White House. Bedtime for Amy was after 11:00 p.m. (Courtesy Jimmy Carter Library.)

EAST ROOM, THE WHITE HOUSE, OCTOBER 1981 (ABOVE) AND NOVEMBER 1981 (BELOW). Singing legend Ella Fitzgerald gives a command performance at a Reagan state dinner for King Juan Carlos I of Spain. As was his custom, Reagan sent Fitzgerald a handwritten thank-you note. "The King and Queen are both fans of American music and they were still talking about you when we put them in their car to Spain," Reagan wrote. "And why not—Nancy and I are still talking about you." Below, musicians Benny Goodman, playing clarinet, and Buddy Rich, playing drums, headlined Pres. Ronald Reagan's state dinner for King Hussein of Jordan. The Reagans are seated to the right. (Both courtesy Ronald Reagan Library.)

GRAND FOYER, THE WHITE HOUSE, MAY 1975. First Lady Betty Ford and world-renowned dancer Edward Villella share a dance (left). Villella was invited to perform at a state dinner for Prime Minister Lee Kuan Yew of Singapore and his wife, Kwa Geok Choo. Immediately after they left, Ford strutted her stuff! Below, Pres. Gerald R. Ford and a beaming First Lady Betty Ford speak with dancer and entertainer Fred Astaire during the state dinner for the Shah of Iran, Mohammad Reza Pahlavi, and the Shahbanou Farah Pahlavi. Betty Ford was a trained dancer and loved to cut a rug whenever possible. (Both courtesy Gerald R. Ford Library.)

STATE DINNER, MAY 1975. First Lady Betty Ford is swept off her feet by Astaire, and one can almost hear the music in her expression: "Heaven, I'm in heaven, and my heart beats so that I can hardly speak." (Courtesy Gerald R. Ford Library.)

East Room, the White House, April 1973. Pres. Richard M. Nixon hosts a state dinner for Giulio Andreotti, president of the Council of Ministers of the Italian Republic. From left to right are Giulio Andreotti, his wife, Livia Andreotti, crooner Frank Sinatra, First Lady Pat Nixon, and President Nixon. When a president wants to impress dinner guests from Italy, he invites the world's most famous Italian American over to sing "I've Got the World on a String." Sinatra came out of "retirement" for the gig. But it was an offer no one could refuse—both Sinatra and Andreotti were notorious for alleged ties to the mafia. (Courtesy National Archives.)

Uline Arena, Washington, D.C., January 1946. Academy Award–winning actor Charles Coburn (left) chats with Adm. Chester Nimitz, chief of naval operations, at the Roosevelt Birthday Ball. In the 1940s, Coburn was an active leader of the Motion Picture Alliance for the Preservation of American Ideals. The group was dedicated to keeping communists out of Hollywood during the cold war. (Courtesy Harry S. Truman Library.)

GRAND FOYER, THE WHITE HOUSE, OCTOBER 1985. Pres. Ronald Reagan and First Lady Nancy Reagan pose with action star Sylvester Stallone and his wife, actress Brigitte Nielsen, during a state dinner for Prime Minister Lee Kuan Yew of Singapore. What better way to impress a head of state than to invite Rocky, Rambo, and his supermodel wife to dinner? (Courtesy Ronald Reagan Library.)

POPE AIR FORCE BASE, FAYETTEVILLE, NORTH CAROLINA, MAY 1987. Pres. Ronald Reagan greets sitcom star Kirk Cameron at the Bob Hope Salute to the United States Air Force 40th Anniversary celebration. Other entertainers include Phyllis Diller, Lucille Ball (center), and Emmanuel Lewis. (Courtesy Ronald Reagan Library.)

SOUTH LAWN, THE WHITE HOUSE, JUNE 1989. Pres. George H. W. Bush and folk singer John Denver pitch a dressed-up round of horseshoes before a state dinner. In the 1980s, Denver was often a vocal critic of the Reagan/Bush administration, but his all-American celebrity status frequently eclipsed politics. He was a sought-after state dinner guest to Republicans Nixon and Bush. (Courtesy George Bush Presidential Library.)

SOUTH LAWN, THE WHITE HOUSE, JUNE 1993. Pres. Bill Clinton jams with famous jazz musicians Illinois Jacquet (left) and Joshua Redman at the Newport Jazz Festival Anniversary performance. As the concert was in full swing, Clinton was handed his sax and called out, "What key are we playing in?" He then spun into a slow blues solo, electrifying the crowd. (Courtesy William J. Clinton Presidential Library.)

FAMILY MOVIE THEATER, THE WHITE HOUSE, JUNE 1994. Hollywood heavyweight Jack Nicholson puts up his feet for a presidential screening of his new film *Wolf*. Pres. Bill Clinton and First Lady Hillary Rodham Clinton are seated next to him. The tagline to the film is, "Inside every man there are two people—one good, one beast." (Courtesy William J. Clinton Presidential Library.)

SOUTH LAWN, THE WHITE HOUSE, AUGUST 1988. Pres. Ronald Reagan and First Lady Nancy Reagan dance with, from left to right, entertainers Stubby Kaye, Shirley Jones, Marvin Hamlisch, and Lee Roy Reams during a rehearsal for *In Performance at the White House*. The Reagans were the stars of the show in Washington—this time, literally. They hosted the televised show and gladly performed for the camera. (Courtesy Ronald Reagan Library.)

SOUTH LAWN, THE WHITE HOUSE, JUNE 1983. Pres. Ronald Reagan and First Lady Nancy Reagan share the stage with the Beach Boys. The all-American pop group was under fire for increasingly raucous Fourth of July concerts on the National Mall. Controversy swirled, threatening to cancel the concert once and for all. The Reagans set out to restore the group's good name—and score some political points—asking them to entertain for the 15th anniversary of the Special Olympics. Reagan remarked, "Our whole family have been fans of yours for a long time, just look at Nancy." Lead singer Mike Love replied, "I can tell that. She's a California girl, what the heck." (Courtesy Ronald Reagan Library.)

WINFIELD HOUSE, LONDON, ENGLAND, JULY 1981. First Lady Nancy Reagan poses with actor Douglas Fairbanks Jr. and actress-turned-princess Grace Kelly during a dinner for Prince Charles and Lady Diana's "Wedding of the Century." After President Reagan's assassination attempt in late March, Nancy Reagan was taking up a heightened interest in astrology—and she was in good company. Grace Kelly was also a firm believer. (Courtesy Ronald Reagan Library.)

THE WHITE HOUSE, JANUARY 1946. Child actress Margaret O'Brien sits between the president's daughter, Margaret Truman, and Pres. Harry S. Truman at the White House during the FDR Birthday Ball. Clockwise from bottom left are Diana Lynn, Angela Lansbury, Helen Sioussat, Eddie Bracken, Paul Henreid, Zachary Scott, Alexis Smith, and Cesar Romero. (Courtesy Harry S. Truman Library.)

CHINA ROOM, THE WHITE HOUSE, APRIL 1990. First Lady Barbara Bush, children's entertainer Sherry Lewis, and puppet Lamb Chop greet Easter visitors, including Margaret Bush (center) holding presidential grandson Walker while granddaughter Marshall gives Lamb Chop a hug. Others are unidentified. Lewis emceed the annual White House Easter Festival for three seasons. A few years later, Lewis and Lamb Chop testified before Congress supporting the Children's Television Act, a law right up their alley—it required stations to provide educational programming. (Courtesy George Bush Presidential Library.)

GRAND FOYER, THE WHITE HOUSE, FEBRUARY 1981.
Pres. Ronald Reagan and First Lady Nancy Reagan share a laugh with comedian Bob Hope during a state dinner for Prime Minister Margaret Thatcher. It was Reagan's first formal meeting with Thatcher since becoming president. Hope was the perfect dinner guest—not only did he help lighten the mood, but the beloved American comedian was born in Great Britain, having left for the United States at the age of four. Later Thatcher delighted a British Embassy crowd with a quip that Hope surely must have left his home country because he "thought the golf courses in the United States were better than those in the United Kingdom." (Both courtesy Ronald Reagan Library.)

THE KENNEDY CENTER, WASHINGTON, D.C., MAY 1983. Pres. Ronald Reagan and First Lady Nancy Reagan pose for a photograph with, from left to right, supermodels Christie Brinkley, Cheryl Tiegs, and Brooke Shields at a tribute for Bob Hope's 80th birthday. The Reagans hosted a show-biz evening filled with star-studded well-wishers, including Lynda Carter, Dudley Moore, and George Burns. (Courtesy Ronald Reagan Library.)

GRAND FOYER, THE WHITE HOUSE, DECEMBER 1999. Pres. Bill Clinton greets actor Robert DeNiro and filmmaker Martin Scorsese for America's Millennium Celebration. The dusk-to-dawn evening was as lavish as it gets—guests at the Millennium Dinner dined on beluga caviar, lobster, oysters, and rack of lamb. Afterward was an extravaganza produced by Quincy Jones featuring fireworks and an 18-minute film premier by Steven Spielberg. Then it was back to the White House for dancing and an early-morning pre-dawn breakfast. (Courtesy William J. Clinton Presidential Library.)

Two

FRIENDS AND PHOTO OPS

The Reagans brought with them a grand circle of celebrity friends, President Obama made several along the way, and both President Bushes enjoyed cutting loose with country music stars and sports champions. Regardless of who sits in the White House, they are always visited and befriended by Hollywood star power. Let's face it: it's lonely at the top. When CBS's 60 *Minutes* interviewed President Obama, he said former presidents advised him "there's a certain loneliness to the job." It's true—who else is your equal when you are leader of the free world? More importantly, who is your friend? An American president is tested on a daily basis; the question is, will he sink or rise to every occasion? This may lend a clue as to why politicians and performers develop meaningful and enduring friendships with one another. The entire world is their audience and all eyes are squarely on them. "At the end of the day there is no difference between Hollywood celebrity and political celebrity," says NBC television writer/producer Jonathan Shapiro. "The same skills that get you all the way to the White House are virtually the same to succeed in Hollywood." They share the same lifestyle, too—both the commander in chief and the captains of the box office get in their limousines, pass by legions of press on their doorstep, and read reviews from their demanding public. Sometimes it is good to have friends who understand a crazy lifestyle—people with whom one can shed the public persona for a moment and have some fun.

Indeed, in the dog-eat-dog world of celebrity and politics, people need to keep their friends close and their enemies closer. It might be hard to distinguish one from the other under the bubble of 24-hour media, paparazzi, and the rumor mill, but that has never stopped anyone from trying. On the pages that follow are images of matches made in heaven—and more than a few strange bedfellows.

VETS AUDITORIUM, DES MOINES, IOWA, DECEMBER 2007. Talk show star Oprah Winfrey was more famous for endorsing books and dieting tips than presidential candidates. But all that changed

at her first official campaign rally for Democratic candidate Barack Obama's run for the White House. (Courtesy Joe Crimmings Photography.)

PRIVATE RESIDENCE, NEW YORK, NEW YORK, MAY 1962. Pres. John F. Kennedy, Attorney General Robert Kennedy, and actress Marilyn Monroe attend a star-studded party at the Manhattan town home of motion picture executive Arthur Krim. Just a few hours prior, Monroe had electrified a Madison Square Garden crowd, singing a seductive version of "Happy Birthday, Mr. President" for Kennedy's 45th birthday gala. Rumors about the nature of her relationship with the president never ceased. (Courtesy John F. Kennedy Presidential Library, Boston.)

CABINET ROOM, THE WHITE HOUSE, JULY 1976. Pres. Gerald Ford meets with Buffalo Bills star running back O. J. Simpson, in town to appear in a bicentennial program at the Kennedy Center. In 2008, Simpson claimed one of his presidential photographs was stolen. He set out to recover the item, confronting two sports memorabilia dealers at gunpoint. Simpson was found guilty of kidnapping and robbery and sentenced to prison. He claimed he just wanted to pass along precious family heirlooms, including his official presidential photograph with President Ford, to his children. (Courtesy Gerald R. Ford Library.)

FAMILY MOVIE THEATER, THE WHITE HOUSE, JUNE 1995. Pres. Bill Clinton addresses a gathering for a private preview of *Apollo 13* as director Ron Howard looks on from the doorway. Hollywood mogul and big-time Clinton contributor Lew Wasserman and his wife, Edie, are the VIPs seated with the First Lady in the first row. (Courtesy William J. Clinton Presidential Library.)

EAST ROOM, THE WHITE HOUSE, DECEMBER 1992. Pres. George H. W. Bush laughs as *Saturday Night Live* alum Dana Carvey does his impression of the president. Carvey and his wife, Paula, were invited to stay the night in the Lincoln bedroom. The comedian could not resist prank calling the Secret Service detail and, in his all-too-perfect Bush impersonation, asked, "Feel like going jogging tonight . . . in the nude?" (Courtesy George Bush Presidential Library.)

LAKESIDE GOLF COURSE, BURBANK, CALIFORNIA, JANUARY 1970. Pres. Richard M. Nixon enjoys a day of golf with comedian Bob Hope and actor Fred MacMurray. During the 1968 election, MacMurray joined Hope and actor Jimmy Stewart in campaigning for Nixon against Hubert Humphrey and third-party candidate George Wallace. (Courtesy National Archives.)

INDOOR SWIMMING POOL, THE WHITE HOUSE, AUGUST 1965. Pres. Lyndon B. Johnson enjoys a swim with, from left to right, Chief of Protocol Lloyd Hand and Special Assistant Jack Valenti. Powerful interests in Hollywood, including Universal Studios mogul Lew Wasserman, lobbied successfully to install Valenti as head of the Motion Picture Association. Valenti reigned there for 38 years and forged an indelible, unprecedented bond between Hollywood and Washington. (Photograph by Yoichi R. Okamoto; courtesy LBJ Library.)

CENTER HALL, THE WHITE HOUSE, FEBRUARY 2000. Pres. Bill Clinton gives a private White House tour to actress Meg Ryan, her then-husband actor Dennis Quaid, and son Jack Quaid at a screening of Ryan's new film *Hanging Up.* After the nearly two-hour tour, Clinton unexpectedly asked the family to stay the night at the White House. They darted back to their hotel to transfer their suitcases. The next day, according to *People* magazine, Quaid changed his flight so he could play a round of golf with new pal Clinton. (Courtesy William J. Clinton Presidential Library.)

PRESIDENTIAL SECRETARY'S OFFICE, THE WHITE HOUSE, NOVEMBER 1962. Actresses Judy Garland (left) and Carol Burnett arrive to see Pres. John F. Kennedy. Garland established a close bond with Kennedy while he was in the Senate. Garland producer Norman Jewison often recounted that Kennedy occasionally liked Garland to phone him and sing "Over the Rainbow" when he needed cheering up but said she need only sing the last eight bars. (Courtesy Cecil Stoughton, White House/John F. Kennedy Presidential Library, Boston.)

OVAL OFFICE, THE WHITE HOUSE, NOVEMBER 1962. President Kennedy meets with, from left to right, composer Richard Adler and entertainers Judy Garland, Carol Burnett, and Danny Kaye. (Courtesy Cecil Stoughton, White House/John F. Kennedy Presidential Library, Boston.)

ANOTHER VIEW OF THE OVAL OFFICE, THE WHITE HOUSE, NOVEMBER 1962. Pres. John F. Kennedy meets with actor Danny Kaye and advisor Dave Powers (actress Carol Burnett is hidden) while screen legend Judy Garland leans against the president's desk enjoying a cigarette. She earned it: Garland traveled the world in support of Kennedy's run for the White House, adding star power and money to his campaign war chest. (Courtesy Cecil Stoughton, White House/John F. Kennedy Presidential Library, Boston.)

PRIVATE RESIDENCE, BEVERLY HILLS, CALIFORNIA, AUGUST 1981. During the 1980 campaign, *Time* magazine quoted one prominent Hispanic leader supporting Carter over Reagan, "If we wanted an actor we would vote for Ricardo Montalban." A year later, President Reagan held a dinner with actor Ricardo Montalban, Charlton Heston, and their wives to celebrate his presidency. The friends gathered at the posh home of Alfred Bloomingdale, heir to the Bloomingdale department store fortune. (Courtesy Ronald Reagan Library.)

DIPLOMATIC RECEPTION ROOM, THE WHITE HOUSE, JUNE 1983. Pres. Ronald Reagan talks with actor Christopher Reeve and sportscaster Frank Gifford during the Special Olympics 15th anniversary. Gifford first met Reagan in 1973 when he invited Reagan and singer/songwriter John Lennon to the booth of *Monday Night Football*. To his shock, both showed up. Gifford recalled, "Ronald Reagan with his arm around John Lennon's shoulder, explaining American football—that's something special." (Courtesy Ronald Reagan Library.)

North Parking Lot, White House Grounds, April 1978. Singer Willie Nelson, with his entourage, chats with Pres. Jimmy Carter. Carter invited Nelson to stay at the White House. According to legend, before turning in, Nelson wandered up to the White House roof to enjoy "a fat Austin torpedo" marijuana cigarette. Nelson told *Blender*, "My short-term memory is so bad I don't remember that. I'll check with Jimmy." Carter later told *Rolling Stone*, "All the mistakes I made [as President]—you can blame half of that on Willie." (Courtesy Jimmy Carter Library.)

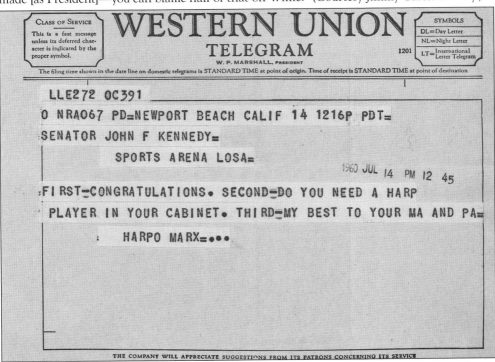

Telegram, Newport Beach, California to Los Angeles, California, July 1960. Comic Harpo Marx telegrams Democratic nominee for Pres. John F. Kennedy moments after his official nomination. Marx (the Marx brother who talked through sounds and instruments) does not beat around the bush vying for a musical cabinet post. (Courtesy National Archives.)

NORTH PORTICO, THE WHITE HOUSE, MAY 1961. Pres. John F. Kennedy and First Lady Jacqueline Kennedy greet Prince Rainier III, Sovereign Prince of Monaco, and Her Serene Highness Princess Grace of Monaco for a luncheon in their honor. Jackie and actress Grace Kelly were remarkably similar—both lived fairy tale lives, both were fashion icons, and both had daughters named Caroline. This day, the glamorous group dined with other invited guests that included movie producers, artists, and politicos. Spring lamb and Dom Perignon topped the exquisite menu. JFK and Grace Kelly had first met in 1954. Then-senator Kennedy was recovering from back surgery; Jackie snuck Grace Kelly into her husband's hospital room wearing a nurse uniform to cheer him up. (Both courtesy Abbie Rowe, White House/John F. Kennedy Presidential Library, Boston.)

UNKNOWN LOCATION, 1976. Sen. John Warner (R-VA) is pictured with his wife, actress Elizabeth Taylor. For Warner, the marriage brought political advantages. Not only did Taylor get Warner wide name recognition for his election; she could attract gobs of campaign cash. Warner's senate career ultimately lasted much longer than his marriage. The couple divorced in 1982, but for Taylor, who married eight times, it was her second longest. (Courtesy U.S. Senate Historical Office.)

OVAL OFFICE, THE WHITE HOUSE, JUNE 1977. Pres. Jimmy Carter is pictured with country star Johnny Cash and family. June Carter Cash was a distant cousin of the president. After this meeting, Carter asked the Cashes to walk with him while going from meeting to meeting around the White House. It was hard for Johnny Cash to keep up with Carter's busy schedule, and after a day full of official events, the singer needed a nap. (Courtesy Jimmy Carter Library.)

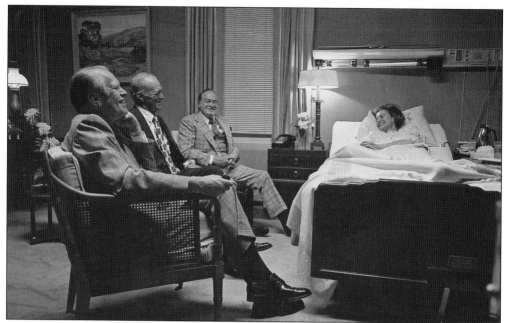

BETHESDA NAVAL HOSPITAL, BETHESDA, MARYLAND, OCTOBER 1974. Pres. Gerald Ford, entertainer Bob Hope, and an unidentified man visit First Lady Betty Ford during her recovery from breast cancer surgery. Betty Ford was in good spirits seeing Hope—and the president was so at ease, he puffed on his pipe. (Courtesy Gerald R. Ford Library.)

ELDORADO COUNTRY CLUB, RANCHO MIRAGE, CALIFORNIA, DECEMBER 1987. Pres. Ronald Reagan poses with actor Kirk Douglas and his wife, Anne Buydens, at a private dinner. Though Douglas recorded a political advertisement for Reagan's opponent in the 1966 campaign for California governor, the actor grew to like Reagan as president. Douglas reflected in his autobiography, *The Ragman's Son,* "Reagan exuded a spirit similar to Kennedy, he got people inspired, excited about their country." (Courtesy Ronald Reagan Library.)

UNIVERSAL STUDIOS, UNIVERSAL CITY, CALIFORNIA, 1940. Fresh out of Harvard, John F. Kennedy signs a copy of his bestselling book, *Why England Slept*, for Spencer Tracy (the book was a published version of Kennedy's senior thesis). Tracy once said, "Actors have no damn place in politics, period." But he did not follow his own advice and attended the Democratic National Convention four years later. After college, Kennedy lived in California, meeting showbiz legends and marveling at how they created powerful public personas. Below, the 23-year-old Kennedy was also interested in getting to know many of Hollywood's hottest leading ladies. Here he meets Margaret Sullivan on the set of her latest picture. (Both courtesy John F. Kennedy Presidential Library, Boston.)

SOUTH LAWN, THE WHITE HOUSE, DECEMBER 2000. Pres. Bill Clinton greets superstar Barbra Streisand and her husband, actor James Brolin, at a National Medal of Arts ceremony. Streisand raised millions for Clinton's campaigns and causes and received scrutiny for her many stays in the Lincoln bedroom. Clinton advisor George Stephanopoulos told the press, "I don't want to give the impression that she's on the White House staff. But when the President speaks to her, he values what she has to say." (Courtesy William J. Clinton Presidential Library.)

WESTERN WHITE HOUSE, SAN CLEMENTE, CALIFORNIA, JULY 1972. Pres. Richard M. Nixon and National Security Adviser Henry Kissinger meet with screen legend John Wayne. Nixon idolized Wayne, and a love of cowboy culture permeated Nixon's White House. Kissinger told *Time* magazine, "The Americans love the cowboy who comes into town all alone on his horse. This romantic and surprising character suits me because being alone has always been part of my style." (Courtesy National Archives.)

Attorney General's Home Phone:
ELmwood 6-7872

May 28, 1964

Miss Judy Garland
Hotel Mandarin
Connaught Road
Central HONG KONG

THINKING OF YOU AND WE WANT YOU TO KNOW HOW MUCH YOU ARE LOVED AND

NEEDED BY ALL OF US. I HAVE NOTIFIED THE NX AMERICAN CONSUL IN HONG KONG

THAT YOU ARE THERE SO LET HIM KNOW IF HE CAN BE OF ANY HELP TO YOU.

IN THE MEANTIME, IF THERE IS ANYTHING WE CAN DO PLEASE GET IN TOUCH

WITH ME.

LOVE,

BOBBY AND ETHEL

TELEGRAMS, WASHINGTON, D.C., AND HONG KONG, MAY AND JUNE 1964. Six months after the death of Pres. John F. Kennedy, Attorney General Robert Kennedy learned of singing icon Judy Garland's failing health and sent her the telegram above. While in Hong Kong, Garland had to get a tracheotomy and was told never to sing again. Nevertheless, her willpower was not broken and she was already planning an inevitable comeback—dramatically writing Kennedy only days later (below) that she felt "stronger every day" and was planning her return. (Both courtesy John F. Kennedy Presidential Library, Boston.)

TELEGRAM
SPECIAL

YWC2425 ZCZC SMU3488 HMM2223 MDO788
HONGKONG 51 7 210S

ATTORNEY GENERAL ROBERT KENNEDY WASHINGTONDC

DEAREST BOBBY GETTING STRONGER EVERY DAY MEDICS ADVISE

NOT LEAVING HONGKONG UNTIL FRIDAY AT LEAST SHALL PROBABLY

PROCEED TO TOKYO ITINERARY CHANGED BECAUSE OF WEATHER BUT

WILL KEEP YOU ADVISED AT ALL TIMES GOD BLESS YOU FOR YOUR

HELP I SEND YOU DEAREST LOVE

JUDY GARLAND

OVAL OFFICE, THE WHITE HOUSE, MAY 1990. Above, Pres. George H. W. Bush greets singing sensation Whitney Houston and her family during the president's Youth Leadership Forum. Sometimes attracting media attention to a good cause is tricky. A forum on community service doesn't generate big headlines, unless you ask America's No. 1 pop and R&B singer to join in. Below, Pres. George H. W. Bush sits with Whitney Houston. Bush's political strategists wanted to aim for 20–25 percent of the African American vote in his reelection campaign. Symbolic photo opportunities such as this with Houston, one of America's greatest black entertainers, were also a shrewd political move. (Both courtesy George Bush Presidential Library.)

OVAL OFFICE, THE WHITE HOUSE, JUNE 1981. Pres. Ronald Reagan and First Lady Nancy Reagan receive a baseball from entertainer Frank Sinatra during a meeting at a national Multiple Sclerosis event. Sinatra dreamed of a sports writing career, and Reagan got his start doing baseball play-by-play on the radio. Perhaps Sinatra was cheering Reagan up—America's baseball players went on strike two weeks later, putting a halt to the season. (Courtesy Ronald Reagan Library.)

U.S. CAPITOL, WASHINGTON, D.C., NOVEMBER 1971. Pictured from left to right are Sen. Hugh Scott (R-PA), unidentified, and entertainers Carol Channing, Jonathan Winters, and Nipsy Russell. The performers were in town for the television show *Festival at Ford's*, an all-star variety show at Ford's Theatre. When stars come to Washington, it is common to double dip—entertain and advocate. While it is not known what cause the entertainers were representing in this photograph, it is sure they drummed up plenty of attention. (Courtesy U.S. Senate Historical Office.)

OVAL OFFICE, THE WHITE HOUSE, MARCH 1973. Entertainer Sammy Davis Jr. visits with Pres. Richard M. Nixon. Davis had been a lifelong Democrat until being tossed from Pres. John F. Kennedy's inaugural lineup. Many speculated it was due to his interracial marriage. So Davis jumped right into Republican politics by warmly supporting Nixon. On this day, Nixon returned the favor by inviting the entertainer to stay the night. Davis was given the royal treatment, staying in the Queen's Bedroom. The *New York Times* reported that, as a result of Nixon's invitation, Sammy Davis Jr. became the first African American ever invited to spend the night in the White House. (Courtesy National Archives.)

OVAL OFFICE, THE WHITE HOUSE, MARCH 1978. Pres. Jimmy Carter greets actor Kirk Douglas and wife Ann Douglas. Douglas developed a close friendship with Carter, but years later, the relationship strained over Carter's 2006 book, *Palestine: Peace Not Apartheid*. (Courtesy Jimmy Carter Library.)

FAMILY RESIDENCE DINING ROOM, THE WHITE HOUSE, MARCH 1978. First Lady Rosalynn Carter hosts a luncheon for actor Kirk Douglas, Anne Douglas, Motion Picture Association chairman Jack Valenti, and Mary Margaret Valenti. Jack Valenti, a former speechwriter for President Johnson, occasionally wrote to Carter offering counsel. He was also notoriously a one-man conduit for Hollywood stars to gain entry to see various presidents for a meeting or a first-class lunch. (Courtesy Jimmy Carter Library.)

PRIVATE RESIDENCE, NEW YORK, NEW YORK, MAY 1962. Pres. John F. Kennedy and actress Shirley MacLaine are at a birthday party for the President. A loyal Democrat, MacLaine was among a throng of celebrities who helped Frank Sinatra's Rat Pack raise money for Kennedy's 1960 campaign. Both MacLaine and Kennedy were named honorary members of the Rat Pack. MacLaine was the only female to earn such titular designation. (Courtesy Cecil Stoughton/John F. Kennedy Presidential Library, Boston.)

GRAND FOYER, THE WHITE HOUSE, MAY 1984. Pres. Ronald Reagan and First Lady Nancy Reagan pose with actor Rock Hudson at a state dinner for Pres. Miguel De La Madrid Hurtado of Mexico. Hudson was secretly grappling with AIDS—a new virus in the 1980s that was not fully understood or acknowledged. When Nancy Reagan noticed Hudson's weight loss, the actor attributed it to a bug picked up overseas. But Hudson died the next year, and his death sparked criticism of Reagan's slow AIDS policy. (Courtesy Ronald Reagan Library.)

Pres. John F. Kennedy chats with comedian Milton Berle, holding his signature stogie. Berle, a notorious cigar aficionado, gave Kennedy a walnut humidor as an inauguration day gift. He commissioned famous cigar maker Alfred Dunhill of London to handcraft the walnut box. Berle affixed a small plaque on it: "To J. F. K. Good Health—Good Smoking. Milton Berle, 1/20/61." (Courtesy John F. Kennedy Presidential Library, Boston.)

U.S. Capitol, Washington, D.C., April 1987. Boxing champ Sugar Ray Leonard visits, from left to right, Senators Pete Wilson (R-CA), Bob Dole (R-KS), and Robert Byrd (D-WV). Leonard grew up just a few miles from the Capitol, discovering in a local gym that he had the right stuff to be a boxing legend—perhaps fitting, because there is may be no better analogy to the battles raging on Capitol Hill than the slugfest of a welterweight boxing match. Judging by the senators' expressions, they understand that all too well. (Courtesy U.S. Senate Historical Office.)

TENNIS COURT, THE WHITE HOUSE, OCTOBER 1990. Pres. George H. W. Bush plays a game of doubles tennis with "king of swing" Pete Sampras. The White House has many outlets for blowing off steam for its overworked occupants: swimming, bowling, horseshoes, a gym, tennis courts, and more. Bush, a tennis fanatic, was hyper-aware of playing a country club sport like tennis out in public. He wanted to avoid looking elitist. As his time in office marched on, Bush had bigger problems—a war in the Middle East and economic pressures. A round of tennis with the No. 1 player in the world was just the ticket to relive some stress. As for Sampras, who was born in Washington, D.C., he seemed right at home. (Courtesy George Bush Presidential Library.)

INVERRARY COUNTRY CLUB, HOLLYWOOD, FLORIDA, FEBRUARY 1975. Pres. Gerald Ford is pictured with comedians Jackie Gleason and Bob Hope at the Jackie Gleason Inverrary Classic, an annual golf tournament for the Boys' Clubs of America. Ford, a golf hound, was a regular on the charity circuit for many years. He loved a pleasant day hitting the links and especially wisecracking with the comics. (Courtesy Gerald R. Ford Library.)

OVAL OFFICE, THE WHITE HOUSE, DECEMBER 1974. President Ford is shown with singer George Harrison and keyboardist Billy Preston. This is a case of what a father will do for a son. The president's son Jack extended an invitation to the rockers for a private lunch at the White House. As their limousines rolled up, reporters shouted questions like "Will the Beatles be getting back together," and "Are you gonna have a rock concert at the White House?" (Courtesy Gerald R. Ford Library.)

OVAL OFFICE, THE WHITE HOUSE, APRIL 1973. Pres. Richard M. Nixon holds an ashtray on the floor, providing the perfect putting cup for comedian Bob Hope. A close friend of Nixon, Hope kept his Republican leanings largely to himself. He always kept the reputation as a bipartisan entertainer, and jokes came at the expense of Democrats and Republicans alike. Still, Hope publicly campaigned and raised money for both of Nixon's presidential elections. (Courtesy National Archives.)

Three

ACTORS TO ACTIVISTS

Sometimes activists happen to become actors and musicians. It happens more than we might think. And why not? It takes a natural drive and outspoken ambition to claw into stardom. So it makes sense that many famous names and faces have something to say—and it's not off a script. Robin Bronk heads the Creative Coalition, the leading political advocacy group for show business. Bronk says nowadays "celebrities need an agent, a manager, a publicist and an issue." Saving the spotted owl or protesting against landmines is not necessarily good for an acting career, but it shows how the power of celebrity can be used for the common good. "There's no need to check your citizenship at the stage door," says Bronk. All of this idealism can come off as goofy to a Washington desk-jockey. But it is wise not to brush it off; celebrities at the top of their game can successfully push an agenda straight through the stuffiest bureaucracy.

Political media sage and songwriter Mark McKinnon notes, "musicians especially almost always represent the anti-establishment, the voice of those without power." Think of activist musicians like Bob Dylan, Bono, and Peter, Paul, and Mary. McKinnon continues, "part of the Hollywood-Washington relationship is finding the art of the possible."

The result of all this goodwill and ambition can lead to some offbeat alliances—exotic film actress Angelina Jolie plots refugee camp security with Sen. Richard Lugar, trailblazing baseball player Jackie Robinson turns up the heat on President Eisenhower for civil rights, and rock star Bono and President Bush buddy up over AIDS policies.

There is plenty of historic evidence that Hollywood is a powerful mouthpiece for political candidates or issues. In World War II, Rita Hayworth, Bing Crosby, and Fred Astaire asked Americans to buy War Bonds to support U.S. forces. Hollywood played a prominent role in the civil rights movement as stars such as Marlon Brando, Paul Newman, and Sammy Davis Jr. led marches on Washington in the 1960s. Dan Glickman sees Hollywood from both the political side and within the film industry as the president and chief executive officer of the Motion Picture Association of America. "When a celebrity shows up at your hearing on Capitol Hill," he notes, "you are guaranteed to have a full room of reporters, staff members—and it usually means more congressmen show up too." Whatever the result, it is always great theater when actors turn into activists.

OVAL OFFICE, THE WHITE HOUSE, OCTOBER 2005. Pres. George W. Bush invites rock star Bono to lunch. Bush and Bono lunched for nearly two hours in the Oval Office dining room discussing global AIDS and Africa policy. Afterward, Bono headed seven blocks away to give a rock concert at Washington's Verizon Center—all in a day's work for a globally conscious rock star. (White House photograph by Eric Draper.)

SAN ANTONIO MUNICIPAL AUDITORIUM, SAN ANTONIO, TEXAS, APRIL 1945. Renowned contralto Marian Anderson entertains a group of overseas veterans. After an Anderson performance was cancelled by the Daughters of the American Revolution on account of her skin color, First Lady Eleanor Roosevelt arranged a concert featuring Anderson for 75,000 of her fans at the Lincoln Memorial, further helping pave the way for equality. (Courtesy National Archives.)

AN KHE, VIETNAM, DECEMBER 1965. Master of the one-liner comedian Bob Hope and Dianne Bates (Miss USA) entertain American troops fighting in Vietnam over Christmas. Hope's first Christmas USO tour was in 1948, performing for the GIs who participated in the Berlin Airlift—he went on tour every Christmas for the next 34 years. His last was a December 1990 tour for troops participating in Operation Desert Shield in Saudi Arabia and Bahrain. (Courtesy National Archives.)

WOMSAN, KOREA, OCTOBER 1950. Bob Hope poses with the men of X Corps. (Department of Defense photograph by Cpl. Alex Klein, army.)

U.S. Capitol, Washington, D.C., June 2004. Sen. Richard Lugar (R-IN) gets to work with actress Angelina Jolie at the U.S. Capitol. At 26, Jolie became a United Nations High Commissioner for Refugees goodwill ambassador. Jolie said she was, "Shocked by what I saw" while filming the Hollywood blockbuster *Lara Croft: Tomb Raider* in Cambodia. She reached out to the U.N. and toured refugee camps in over 20 countries. She also founded the Jolie-Pitt Foundation, with husband Brad Pitt, which raised millions for aid workers in trouble spots such as the Darfur region of Sudan. (Both courtesy Office of Senator Richard Lugar.)

LINCOLN MEMORIAL, WASHINGTON, D.C., AUGUST 1963. Folk singers Joan Baez and Bob Dylan are pictured above at the civil rights March on Washington. The historic event inspired Dylan to write "The Times They Are A'Changin'," featuring a direct appeal to Washington: "Come senators, congressmen / Please heed the call / Don't stand in the doorway / Don't block up the hall." Less than a year later, the Civil Rights Act became law. Below, actress and singer Lena Horne joined the March on Washington. Horne's public commitment to civil rights started when she became the first African American signed to a long-term studio contract. She mixed her talent with activism by performing at rallies throughout the country for the National Council for Negro Women. (Both courtesy National Archives.)

UNITEL VIDEO, NEW YORK, NEW YORK, OCTOBER 1989. First Lady Barbara Bush appears with Big Bird on *Sesame Street*. Bush vigorously promoted literacy and reading as First Lady. Proving national activists can be Muppets, too, Bush read Ezra Jack Keats's book *Peter's Chair* to Big Bird, the Count, and the *Sesame Street* neighborhood kids. (Courtesy George Bush Presidential Library.)

U.S. ARMY FORWARD OPERATING BASE FENTY, JALALABAD, AFGHANISTAN, MAY 2007. Country music star Toby Keith and his band perform for U.S. soldiers during a USO tour for coalition forces. Keith, whose father was a U.S. Army veteran, made numerous swings through war-torn countries to boost morale of American troops fighting after the terrorist attacks of September 11, 2001. (U.S. Army photograph by Pfc. Daniel M. Rangel.)

TAL AFAR, NEAR MOSUL, IRAQ, SEPTEMBER 2003. Hollywood action star and singer Bruce Willis brings blues to soldiers of the 101st Airborne Division (Air Assault). Willis launched the Bruce Willis and the Accelerators Touch of Home Tour, telling the press, "I didn't see enough people coming out here and supporting the troops." Being surrounded by soldiers is nothing new for Willis. He was born on a military base in Germany in 1955. (Department of Defense photograph by Pfc. Thomas Day.)

LINCOLN MEMORIAL, WASHINGTON, D.C., AUGUST 1963. Actor Charlton Heston and singer Harry Belafonte support Pres. John F. Kennedy's civil rights bill at the civil rights March on Washington. Heston remarked in speeches that he supported civil rights "long before Hollywood found it fashionable." Below, Belafonte and Heston review a speech for the crowd of 250,000. While Dr. Martin Luther King Jr. rewrote history with his famous speech, many others—including these celebrities—got their 15-minute opportunity at history during the march. (Both courtesy National Archives.)

Oval Office, the White House, May 1996. Actor Christopher Reeve lobbies Pres. Bill Clinton and First Lady Hillary Clinton for spinal research funding. Reeve, recently paralyzed in a horse-riding accident, was emerging as a national advocate for spinal cord research. The Clintons asked the actor to speak at the Democratic National Committee in August. His convention speech aired on prime-time television and captivated the country. (Courtesy William J. Clinton Presidential Library.)

Donovan Hotel, Washington, D.C., January 2009. Actresses Susan Sarandon (center) and Ellen Burstyn (right) attend the Creative Coalition's VIP dinner for President Obama's inauguration. Sarandon founded the Hollywood political advocacy group the Creative Coalition, was appointed a UNICEF ambassador, and was an outspoken critic of the Iraq War, among other things. The actress famously proclaimed she would move to Canada if John McCain won the 2008 election—not to bother, she stayed put in Manhattan. (Courtesy the Creative Coalition.)

FIFTH MARINE DIVISION, SASEBO, JAPAN, OCTOBER 1945. Stage and screen star Danny Kaye entertains occupation troops near a surrender of an Imperial Japanese naval station. A-list performers weren't globetrotting and morale-boosting exclusively for high-ranking officers—the crude sign across the front of the stage says it all: "Officers keep out! Enlisted men's country." (Department of Defense photograph by Pfc. H. J. Grimm, Marine Corps.)

OVAL OFFICE, THE WHITE HOUSE, SEPTEMBER 1972. Singer Ray Charles bends the ear of Pres. Richard M. Nixon about one of his pet causes: greater sickle-cell anemia research. Nixon recently signed the National Sickle Cell Anemia Control Act—a ray of light amid grappling with Vietnam and covering up the Watergate scandal. During such dark days, Nixon loved inviting cherished entertainers like Frank Sinatra, Johnny Cash, James Brown, and numerous sports greats into his Oval Office for a friendly chat. (Both courtesy National Archives.)

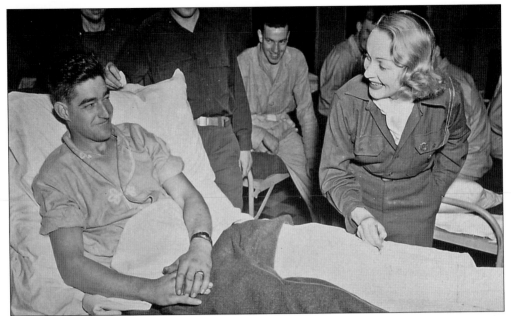

U.S. ARMY FIELD HOSPITAL, BELGIUM, NOVEMBER 1944. Actress Marlene Dietrich autographs the cast of a wounded World War II soldier. German-born Dietrich recorded a number of anti-Nazi propaganda records for America's Office of Strategic Services (the early CIA). Though the Nazi government tried banning the recordings, Germans couldn't get enough of Dietrich, and the government caved. Dietrich would later say such work was her proudest moment. (Courtesy National Archives.)

VICE PRESIDENT'S OFFICE, THE WHITE HOUSE, FEBRUARY 2009. Vice President Joe Biden discusses the conflict in Darfur with actor George Clooney. Having completed a trip to refugee camps on the Sudanese-Chadian border region and then skipping the previous night's Academy Awards, Clooney pressed issues such as appointing a special envoy to Darfur. His work paid off—initially only scheduled to meet with Biden, he was joined by Pres. Barack Obama for an impromptu meeting. The Academy Award–winning actor said the 250,000 living in refugee camps are "hanging on by the skin of their teeth." (White House photograph by Sharon Farmer.)

U.S. CAPITOL, WASHINGTON, D.C., 1970s.
Actor and conservationist Robert Redford
meets with Sen. Charles Percy (R-IL).
During the time of this photograph, rumors
spread that Redford was considering
a run for the Senate in Utah. With
proceeds from his many successful films,
he determined he could make more
environmental impact by buying huge
swaths of Utah land and conserving it
himself. The result was Sundance on
the east side of Mount Timpanogos,
named after Redford's character in *Butch
Cassidy and the Sundance Kid.* (Courtesy
U.S. Senate Historical Office.)

**LINCOLN MEMORIAL, WASHINGTON, D.C.,
AUGUST 1963.** Never to be outdone by his
Butch Cassidy costar, actor Paul Newman
marches in solidarity for civil rights in the
March on Washington. Most came by bus,
but Newman took a private plane from Los
Angeles. (Courtesy National Archives.)

LINCOLN MEMORIAL, WASHINGTON, D.C., AUGUST 1963. Actor Marlon Brando is pictured at the civil rights March on Washington. Brando participated in the "freedom rides," protests that publicly tested segregation court decisions in the South. After the death of Martin Luther King Jr., Brando scrapped his upcoming movie, telling *The Joey Bishop Show*, "I felt I'd better go find out . . . what it is to be black in this country; what this rage is all about." Below, Marlon Brando poses at the march with author and playwright James Baldwin. (Both courtesy National Archives.)

YELLOW OVAL ROOM, THE WHITE HOUSE, MAY 1981. Pres. Ronald Reagan talks with legendary actress Audrey Hepburn and companion Robert Wolders at a private dinner for the Prince of Wales. As a girl, Hepburn was malnourished growing up in Nazi-occupied Holland. It is what drove her to become a tireless UNICEF ambassador. "If a child falls down," she once said, "you pick it up. It's that simple." (Courtesy Ronald Reagan Presidential Library.)

LINCOLN MEMORIAL, WASHINGTON, D.C., AUGUST 1963. Entertainer Sammy Davis Jr. waves to the crowd of 250,000 gathered to hear Dr. Martin Luther King Jr. at the civil rights March on Washington. (Courtesy National Archives.)

THE ELMS, NEWPORT, RHODE ISLAND, SEPTEMBER 1962. Below, First Lady Jacqueline Kennedy views models of the National Cultural Center to be constructed on the banks of the Potomac. In the crowd are actor Danny Kaye, actress Joanne Woodward, and her husband, actor Paul Newman. The first lady was mixing a little business with pleasure while vacationing at her family home, Hammersmith Farm, Rhode Island, while the president was away. Above, actress Geraldine Page unveils architectural plans for the National Cultural Center (later to be named the Kennedy Center). (Both courtesy Cecil Stoughton, White House/John F. Kennedy Presidential Library and Museum, Boston.)

FORT SAM HOUSTON, SAN ANTONIO, TEXAS, JANUARY 2007. Singer-songwriter John Mellencamp is backstage at opening ceremonies for one of the most advanced rehabilitation centers for wartime amputees and burn victims. Mellencamp proclaimed, "It shows the spirit of what people can do on their own when they want to and when they need to." (Department of Defense photograph by S.Sgt. D. Myles Cullen.)

NATIONAL MALL, WASHINGTON, D.C., AUGUST 1963. Peter, Paul, and Mary sing the Bob Dylan song "Blowin' in the Wind" at the civil rights March on Washington. The lyrics say, "The answer, my friend, is blowin' in the wind," and on this day, the wind carried Dr. Martin Luther King Jr.'s historic speech to the ears of the entire nation. (Courtesy National Archives.)

CHOW HALL, MARSHALL ISLANDS, NOVEMBER 1944. Entertainer Betty Hutton embarks on a 50,000-mile tour of World War II army camps across the South Pacific. The tenacious actress ultimately performed for over two million servicemen. Months earlier, she kicked off the 20-city Hollywood Bond Cavalcade tour, featuring stars Judy Garland, Mickey Rooney, Lucille Ball, Fred Astaire, James Cagney, and Harpo Max. The tour helped raise $18 billion for American forces. (Courtesy National Archives.)

STAGE DOOR CANTEEN, PICCADILLY, LONDON, AUGUST 1944. Wartime crooner Bing Crosby sings to Allied troops at the opening of the Stage Door Canteen. By November 1945, Stage Door Canteens operated in eight U.S. cities, London, and Paris. They brought much-needed downtime for troops, and entertainment lineups included greats like Judy Garland, Glen Miller, and Fred Astaire. (Courtesy National Archives.)

THE PENTAGON, ARLINGTON, VIRGINIA, MAY 2006. Actor Gary Sinise and the Lt. Dan Band kick off the second annual "America Supports You" concert saluting American troops fighting in Iraq and Afghanistan. The Lt. Dan Band gets its name from Sinise's character in *Forrest Gump* (Forrest's best pal, a Vietnam veteran and amputee). Sinise also cofounded Operation Iraqi Children, an effort to help educate Iraq's war-stricken children. (Department of Defense photograph by Helene C. Stikkel.)

EAST WING CORRIDOR, THE WHITE HOUSE, DECEMBER 1981. First Lady Nancy Reagan confers with actor Warren Beatty and actress Diane Keaton. Though the pair were outspoken Democrats, they held a presidential screening of their epic film *Reds*. Beatty directed and starred in the romance set against the Communist revolution. President Reagan watched very few films in the White House theater, preferring instead to watch movies casually on weekends at Camp David. (Courtesy Ronald Reagan Library.)

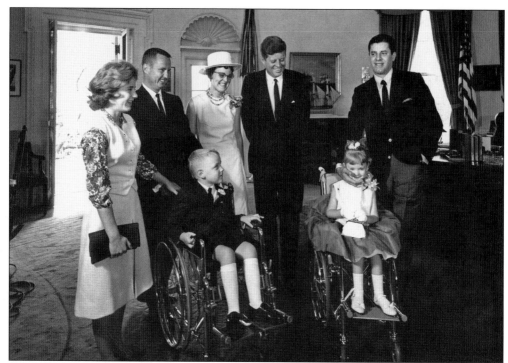

Oval Office, the White House, June 1963. Pres. John F. Kennedy, actress and Muscular Dystrophy Association youth chairperson Patty Duke (left), and MDA chairman Jerry Lewis (right) host poster children Rob (7) and Kerri Whitaker (6), a brother and sister both suffering from the disease. The kids were enamored of Duke, popular star of *The Patty Duke Show*. Kerri recalled, "She . . . didn't seem like a star or a celebrity. She was just like a normal teenager." (Courtesy Abbie Rowe, White House/John F. Kennedy Presidential Library, Boston.)

East Room, the White House, May 1978. Pres. Jimmy Carter and First Lady Rosalynn Carter host a USO reception for Bob Hope; also pictured is Gen. Michael S. Davison, president of the USO, and his wife, Jean Miller Davison. Strengthening the spirit and morale of U.S. troops was Hope's second career, and his work spanned many presidents. (Courtesy Jimmy Carter Library.)

EAST ROOM, THE WHITE HOUSE, MARCH 1998. Actor and executive producer Tom Hanks premieres his miniseries *From the Earth to the Moon* for Pres. Bill Clinton and First Lady Hillary Clinton. John F. Kennedy Jr. (seated beside Hillary Clinton in the front row) was an honored guest to celebrate the legacy of his father's space program. Also attending were the 12 living astronauts who walked on the moon. Hanks set out to chronicle the spirit of America's space program and document the historic achievements of astronauts. (Courtesy William J. Clinton Presidential Library.)

OVAL OFFICE, THE WHITE HOUSE, MAY 1957. Pres. Dwight Eisenhower converses with Jackie Robinson, the first African American to officially play in Major League Baseball, and comedian Joe E. Brown. Robinson broke the color barrier in professional baseball and was determined to take his case for civil rights to the highest office in the land. The late 1950s were an especially sensitive time (as evidenced by the letter on the next page), and perhaps Robinson brought Brown along to lighten the mood. (Courtesy National Park Service, Dwight D. Eisenhower Presidential Library.)

LETTER FROM
JACKIE ROBINSON
TO PRESIDENT
EISENHOWER, MAY
1958. One year after
his visit to the White
House, Robinson
kept the pressure
on Eisenhower,
championing civil
rights from his position
as a leading executive
of the Chock Full o'
Nuts Corporation.
In this letter, he
directs a personal plea
to Eisenhower for
stronger demonstration
of support for black
Americans. (Both
courtesy of the
Dwight D. Eisenhower
Presidential Library.)

Telephone
MUrray Hill 2-0500

Chock full o' Nuts

425 LEXINGTON AVENUE
New York 17, N. Y.

THE WHITE HOUSE
MAY 14 11 36 AM '58
RECEIVED

May 13, 1958

The President
The White House
Washington, D. C.

My dear Mr. President:

I was sitting in the audience at the Summit Meeting of Negro
Leaders yesterday when you said we must have patience. On
hearing you say this, I felt like standing up and saying, "Oh
no! Not again."

I respectfully remind you sir, that we have been the most
patient of all people. When you said we must have self-
respect, I wondered how we could have self-respect and re-
main patient considering the treatment accorded us through
the years.

17 million Negroes cannot do as you suggest and wait for the
hearts of men to change. We want to enjoy now the rights
that we feel we are entitled to as Americans. This we cannot do unless we pursue aggressively goals which all other
Americans achieved over 150 years ago.

As the chief executive of our nation, I respectfully suggest
that you unwittingly crush the spirit of freedom in Negroes
by constantly urging forbearance and give hope to those pro-
segregation leaders like Governor Faubus who would take
from us even those freedoms we now enjoy. Your own experience with Governor Faubus is proof enough that forbearance and not eventual integration is the goal the pro-
segregation leaders seek.

In my view, an unequivocal statement backed up by action
such as you demonstrated you could take last fall in deal-

MAY 26 1958

The President   Page 2   May 13, 1958

ing with Governor Faubus if it became necessary, would let
it be known that America is determined to provide -- in the
near future -- for Negroes -- the freedoms we are entitled to under the constitution.

Respectfully yours,

Jackie Robinson

Jackie Robinson

JR:cc

KIST, GERMANY, APRIL 1945 (ABOVE), AND KOREA, OCTOBER 1952 (BELOW). Private first class and actor Mickey Rooney entertains fellow troops during his service in World War II. Above, he imitates Hollywood actors for an appreciative audience of infantrymen of the 44th Division. Rooney, who served under army general George S. Patton Jr. for three months, would return to the front lines again as a lifelong entertainer for the USO. Below, in 1952, Rooney returned to duty—this time with his USO troupe working the chow line during the Korean War. (Both courtesy National Archives.)

Four

PRESIDENTIAL PRIZES

The Queen of England confers a knighthood, the French bestow the auspicious title of Officier de la Legion d'Honneur for excellence in arts and letters, and Americans have their own special pedestal to honor high achievers. Politicians handing out awards is nothing new. Pres. George Washington gave out medals to Native American nations to preserve the peace. Today one might see medals being awarded to great scientists, architects, or perhaps a rock star. "National awards honoring the greatest achievers represent the architecture of our history and soul," says Mark McKinnon. "They remind us there is something much greater in this country than just politics."

Celebrities rarely shy away from an accolade, and politicians love giving them. Entertainers of all stripes are honored at ceremonies such as the Kennedy Center Honors, the awarding the congressional or presidential medals, or sometimes a plain old presidential slap on the back.

There are ripples in the road. Awards and politics can make for awkward pairings—such as conservative Pres. George W. Bush giving liberal Barbra Streisand a Kennedy Center Honor and a kiss on the cheek. Such couplings make even a seemingly sunny occasion like a medal ceremony produce storm clouds. "Sometimes the president and the recipient are on opposite political sides, and you would think that might complicate matters," says Don Mischer, who has produced many Kennedy Center Honors. "But these occasions end up being about coming back together as a country, celebrating human achievement."

When Muhammad Ali received the Presidential Medal of Freedom, eyebrows were raised; after all, Ali made waves in the 1960s when he very publicly dodged the Vietnam draft. But the award came to symbolize the way time can heal the wounds of a nation, a war, and ultimately a prize fighter. "A lot of our national history is filled with redemption," adds McKinnon.

So a presidential prize can have a meaning every bit as much to the American audience as it does to the recipient. After all, talent isn't finally and "officially" embraced until one receives presidential-level platitudes from a grateful nation.

OVAL OFFICE, THE WHITE HOUSE, APRIL 1990. Pres. George H. W. Bush greets "King of Pop" Michael Jackson to present the Artist of the Decade Award. Bush commended Jackson for amassing a "tremendous following" and for his philanthropic activities for children. Through the 1980s and 1990s, Jackson remained a presidential favorite, appearing at Pres. Bill Clinton's inaugural gala. (Courtesy George Bush Presidential Library.)

OVAL OFFICE, THE WHITE HOUSE, APRIL 1978. Pres. Jimmy Carter receives a handmade Cherokee Indian headdress from "Iron Eyes" Cody. Cody was one of America's first Native American stars, having played in hundreds of films. One of his most profound appearances came in a public service announcement showing the terrible effects of pollution on the American landscape. As a passing car tosses a piece of garbage, it lands in front of teary-eyed Cody. It became the most widely seen public service announcement in history. Cody understood the illusion of Hollywood well. It was later discovered that "Iron Eyes" was born Espera DeCorti to Italian emigrants from Sicily. He traded in his Italian heritage for a career as a beloved American Indian. (Courtesy Jimmy Carter Library.)

NORTH LAWN, THE WHITE HOUSE, JUNE 1985. Pres. Ronald Reagan poses with race car driver Richard Petty and his wife, Lynda. In 1984, Reagan became the first sitting U.S. president to attend a NASCAR race, as he watched Petty's 200th win at the Firecracker 400 in Daytona. The president gave the "gentleman start your engines" command to start the race by phone from Air Force One. Petty summed up a big reason politicians and celebrities often mix: "The President put racing on the front page and we put him on the sports page. You couldn't have written a script for that." (Courtesy Ronald Reagan Presidential Library.)

OVAL OFFICE, THE WHITE HOUSE, JUNE 1986. Pres. Ronald Reagan and pro golfer Raymond Floyd meet after Floyd won the U.S. Open. Golf was a game favored by many of Reagan's friends in Hollywood, and he lamented that, with added Secret Service, it was increasingly hard to hit the links. Like many of his predecessors, Reagan found time for a quick putting match on the Oval Office carpet. (Courtesy Ronald Reagan Library.)

OVAL OFFICE, THE WHITE HOUSE, FEBRUARY 1955. Pres. Dwight Eisenhower presents famous composer Irving Berlin a Congressional Gold Medal. From left to right are treasury secretary George Humphrey, Irving Berlin, President Eisenhower, and Ellin Berlin. Meeting then-general Eisenhower during World War II inspired Berlin to pen the tune "I Like Ike." The song was widely used during Eisenhower's landslide 1952 presidential campaign. (Courtesy National Park Service, Dwight D. Eisenhower Presidential Library.)

BLUE ROOM, THE WHITE HOUSE DECEMBER 2006. Pres. George W. Bush and First Lady Laura Bush host Kennedy Center honorees at a reception. From left to right are singer Smokey Robinson, theatrical composer Andrew Lloyd Webber, country singer Dolly Parton, director Steven Spielberg, and conductor Zubin Mehta. The Kennedy Center Honors have been called Washington's version of the Academy Awards. (White House photograph by Eric Draper.)

SENATE DINING ROOM, U.S. CAPITOL, MARCH 1968. From left to right, Sen. Edmund Muskie (D-ME) and Sen. (and actor) George Murphy (R-CA) attend a luncheon honoring canine sensation Lassie for the dog's "environmentalism." In early 1968, President Johnson signed an environmental bill unofficially dubbed "the Lassie program." No fictional television program taught more valuable lessons about the great outdoors than *Lassie*. The show used national forests as scenery for the heroic stories of young Timmy and his faithful dog Lassie. (U.S. Senate Historical Office.)

STATE DINING ROOM, THE WHITE HOUSE, OCTOBER 1985. First Lady Nancy Reagan congratulates, from left to right, banker G. Chris Anderson, actor Tom Cruise, Olympian Bruce Jenner, pop singer Cher, financier Richard C. Strauss, and artist Robert Rauschenberg. The group was honored by Washington, D.C.'s Lab School for Outstanding Learning Disabled Achievement. All were great successes, overcoming learning disabilities in life. Tom Cruise and Cher, both dyslexics, began dating after meeting one another at the event. Cher was 36; Cruise was 20. (Courtesy Ronald Reagan Library.)

NORTH PORTICO, THE WHITE HOUSE, NOVEMBER 1946. First Lady Bess Truman receives a Community Chest Award with actress Ingrid Bergman (second from right). Truman caused a stir when she attended Bergman's play *Joan of Lorraine* at Washington's Lisner Auditorium. The auditorium was segregated, like much of Washington at the time. Less than a year later, most theaters in Washington reversed their segregation policies. (Courtesy Harry S. Truman Library.)

YELLOW OVAL ROOM, THE WHITE HOUSE, DECEMBER 1981. Pres. Ronald Reagan and movie stars Cary Grant (left) and Douglas Fairbanks Jr. (right) attend a dinner party. Grant was in town to receive a Kennedy Center Honor; and Fairbanks, who starred with Grant in *Gunga Din*, paid tribute. Perhaps neither star ever imagined their fellow actor and friend Reagan would be the president who would one day hand out the prestigious award. (Courtesy Ronald Reagan Library.)

EAST ROOM, THE WHITE HOUSE, SEPTEMBER 1990. Pres. George H. W. Bush and First Lady Barbara Bush present the National Medal of the Arts to opera star Beverly Sills. She had already received the Presidential Medal of Freedom from Jimmy Carter and ever since had focused on making opera more accessible to all. (Courtesy George Bush Presidential Library.)

ROSE GARDEN, THE WHITE HOUSE, SEPTEMBER 1963. Pres. John F. Kennedy and Sen. Stuart Symington (D-MO) present comedian Bob Hope with the Congressional Gold Medal. Legislation to give the rarely awarded medal to Hope crossed all party lines and ideologies for his tireless dedication to entertaining U.S. forces overseas. In customary fashion, Hope closed the ceremony by quipping, "Which way is the golf course?" (Courtesy Abbie Rowe, White House/John F. Kennedy Presidential Library, Boston.)

ROSE GARDEN, THE WHITE HOUSE, SEPTEMBER 1965. Pres. Lyndon B. Johnson, Edward Steichen, and Joanna Steichen are pictured at the signing of the Arts and Humanities Bill, creating the National Endowment for the Arts. For his part, Steichen honed much of his artistic growth through service to the country, leading major military photographic divisions during World War I and World War II. His war documentary *The Fighting Lady* won an Oscar. (Photograph by Yoichi R. Okamoto; courtesy LBJ Library.)

ROSE GARDEN, THE WHITE HOUSE, JUNE 1985. Pres. Ronald Reagan hosts 7-foot, 2-inch NBA champion Kareem Abdul Jabbar and his Los Angeles Lakers teammates. Jabbar not only had to duck to speak into the microphone, he bowed to enter the Oval Office. *The New York Times* reported that Reagan joked, "He didn't have to bow—I'm President not King." (Courtesy Ronald Reagan Library.)

EAST ROOM, THE WHITE HOUSE, NOVEMBER 2005. Pres. George W. Bush presents the Presidential Medal of Freedom to actor Andy Griffith. Said Bush, "TV shows come and go, but there's only one Andy Griffith." (White House photograph by Paul Morse.)

STATE FLOOR, THE WHITE HOUSE, DECEMBER 1996. Pres. Bill Clinton bestows a Kennedy Center Honor on country singer Johnny Cash. Cash made friends with many presidents—especially Nixon. In Cash's autobiography, the singer recalled the Clintons giving him a tour of the ornately decorated White House Christmas trees. He noted he very much liked Hillary Clinton. "I like her husband too," he wrote, "even if I never voted for him. Come to think of it, I didn't vote for Nixon, either." (Courtesy William J. Clinton Presidential Library.)

RENO-SPARKS CONVENTION AND VISITORS CENTER, RENO, NEVADA, AUGUST 2006. Defense secretary Donald Rumsfeld meets with imposing Southern rocker Charlie Daniels during the Veterans of Foreign Wars convention. Both Rumsfeld and Daniels received awards from the VFW for their work with U.S. armed forces. (Department of Defense photograph by S.Sgt. D. Myles Cullen, U.S. Air Force.)

OVAL OFFICE, THE WHITE HOUSE, APRIL 1989. Pres. George H. W. Bush receives a Dallas Cowboys jacket and helmet from team owner Jerry Jones. A maverick oil tycoon, Jones had only owned the team for two months but was already making headlines, firing iconic coach Tom Landry, installing head coach Jimmy Johnson, and boasting about a Super Bowl ring. Jones marched his publicity parade right into the White House to see Texan and fellow oilman Bush. (Courtesy George Bush Presidential Library.)

THE WHITE HOUSE, DECEMBER 1974. First Lady Betty Ford scoops up a signed basketball presented by Harlem Globetrotters player George "Meadowlark" Lemon. The Globetrotters averaged over 250 games a year and starred in movies, a weekly cartoon, and television variety show. They were also heavily involved in charity work with handicapped kids. On this visit, Pres. Gerald and Betty Ford awarded the team a special Presidential Citation. (Courtesy Gerald R. Ford Library.)

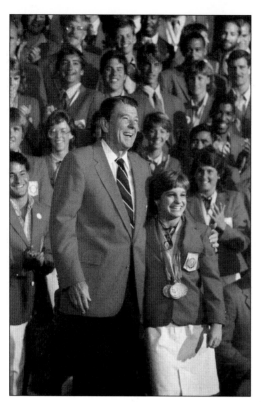

CENTURY PLAZA HOTEL, LOS ANGELES, AUGUST 1984. Pres. Ronald Reagan poses with gold medal winner Mary Lou Retton and the 1984 U.S. Olympic team. Athlete-of-the-year Retton was an outspoken supporter of Reagan. A dedicated Christian conservative, she even appeared in television advertisements supporting him. (Courtesy Ronald Reagan Library.)

SOUTH LAWN, THE WHITE HOUSE, FEBRUARY 1988. President Reagan hosts Super Bowl champions the Washington Redskins before a raucous local crowd of 600,000 fans. Reagan, keen on playing to the audience, asked, "Where's Ricky Sanders?" Then Reagan launched a pass to the star wide receiver across the south lawn. (Courtesy Ronald Reagan Library.)

SOUTH LAWN, THE WHITE HOUSE, JULY 2008. Pres. George W. Bush hosts a tee ball game with country singer Kenny Chesney, Hall of Famer Frank Robinson, and Postmaster General Jack Potter. Avid baseball fan Bush built a stadium on the White House lawn and invited baseball legends to watch kids from all 50 states in action. Chesney sang "Take Me Out to the Ballgame," and Robinson unveiled a new postage stamp commemorating the song's 100th anniversary. (White House photograph by Eric Draper.)

GOVERNOR'S MANSION, JACKSON, MISSISSIPPI, FEBRUARY 2005. Blues great B. B. King wrote "The Thrill Is Gone," but on this day, it came roaring back as Gov. Haley Barbour (R-MS) proclaimed "B. B. King Day." King was speechless during the ceremony. "I never learned to talk very well without Lucille," he said, referring to his trademark black guitar, "I am so happy." (Courtesy Office of Gov. Haley Barbour.)

ROSE GARDEN, THE WHITE HOUSE, JANUARY 1989. In the film *Knute Rockne, All American*, Ronald Reagan played the role of Notre Dame football legend George "The Gipper" Gipp. From then on, Reagan was known as "the Gipper." Here, in one of his last official appearances, Reagan receives George Gipp's university sweater from the Notre Dame football team, who were also that year's national champions. (Courtesy Ronald Reagan Library.)

KENNEDY CENTER, WASHINGTON, D.C., DECEMBER 1987. Pres. Ronald Reagan stands with actress Bette Davis at the Kennedy Center Honors. Davis unconventionally nominated herself for the award, and Reagan decided the screen legend deserved it. "Life is so ironic," said Davis. "Back in our [Warner Brothers] days, who would have thought that little Ronnie Reagan would end up as President and would be presenting me with a medal at the White House? Never in a million years!" (Courtesy Ronald Reagan Library.)

OVAL OFFICE, THE WHITE HOUSE, JULY 1995. Pres. Bill Clinton and actor Tom Hanks pose with Apollo 13 astronaut Jim Lovell, who was awarded the Congressional Space Medal of Honor. Lovell was commander of the Apollo 13 mission, made infamous by Hank's blockbuster film *Apollo 13*. Hanks played Lovell in the film, and the powerful performance earned Hanks an Academy Award nomination. (Courtesy William J. Clinton Presidential Library.)

OVAL OFFICE, THE WHITE HOUSE, SEPTEMBER 1978. Cincinnati Reds third baseman Pete Rose brings his family to meet Pres. Jimmy Carter. In 1978, Rose was fast on his way to becoming a baseball legend. His meteoric rise was tarnished with accusations of gambling. Carter remained a faithful Rose defender, saying, "Evidence about him specifically betting on baseball is less than compelling." Rose was convicted and later confessed. (Courtesy Jimmy Carter Library.)

OVAL OFFICE, THE WHITE HOUSE, OCTOBER 2000. Pres. Bill Clinton chats with, from left to right, unidentified and comic writers and performers Carl Reiner, his son Rob Reiner, and Jerry Seinfeld. Clinton presented Carl Reiner with the Kennedy Center's Mark Twain Prize. A big televised ceremony was held the night before, but Clinton asked Reiner and his friends to the Oval Office for a more personal meeting. Though there was a presidential helicopter waiting outside, Clinton did not leave until he had talked to each and every person in the room—including Reiner's extended family. (Courtesy William J. Clinton Presidential Library.)

BLUE ROOM, THE WHITE HOUSE, MARCH 1984. Acting legend James Cagney talks to his longtime friend Pres. Ronald Reagan and First Lady Nancy Reagan before receiving the Presidential Medal of Freedom. Cagney was a founder of the Screen Actors Guild, which Reagan headed for five terms. (Courtesy Ronald Reagan Library.)

KENNEDY CENTER, WASHINGTON, D.C., DECEMBER 1985. Pres. Ronald Reagan and Bob Hope laugh with George Shultz. Hope had received nearly every award Washington could offer, but he was more than happy to accept the Life Achievement Award at the Kennedy Center Honors. (Courtesy Ronald Reagan Library.)

BLUE ROOM, THE WHITE HOUSE, DECEMBER 2005. Pres. George W. Bush and First Lady Laura Bush pose with Kennedy Center honorees, from left to right, actress Julie Harris, actor Robert Redford, singer Tina Turner, ballet dancer Suzanne Farrell, and singer Tony Bennett. Redford, an outspoken liberal activist, debated whether to accept the award if it was to be presented by conservative Bush. But the Kennedy Center Honors is a once-in-a-lifetime offer. The Oscar-winning actor accepted his award and shook Bush's hand, just as arch conservative Charlton Heston shook President Clinton's hand during the 1997 Kennedy Center Honors. Later in the evening, Bush lightened the mood, proclaiming Tina Turner had "the most famous legs in show business." (White House photograph by Eric Draper.)

Five

PERSONALITIES, POLITICS, AND POWER

Somehow late-night talk shows became a logical first step for politicians to reach voters. Somehow rock stars became a political voice of the disenfranchised. Somewhere along the way, American politics and pop culture personalities began to blend. Blame it on Ike letting cameras into the White House and perhaps Clinton blowing his sax on *The Arsenio Hall Show*—"celebrity creep" into American politics seems to spread over time. Each campaign and each candidate changes the rules, receiving endorsements from big stars and taking lots and lots of their money. It is commonplace for celebrities to stump for candidates, throw lavish fund-raisers, and donate mountains of their own cash. Television advertisement wars, funding a "ground game," and connecting with voters takes big money. And there is lots of "gold in them hills"—Beverly Hills! Bottomless wells of cash await that can make or break a candidate's chance at success.

Glamorous Hollywood stars helped Truman and Eisenhower kick-start national optimism after World War II. Fleetwood Mac's hit "Don't Stop (Thinking about Tomorrow)" became a powerful refrain for Pres. Bill Clinton's 1992 campaign. Perhaps no campaign involved as many vocal celebrities as President Obama's 2008 race for president. There was a day when a candidate may have thought hanging around with rock stars sent the wrong signal. When that star is someone like heartland rocker Bruce Springsteen, it might send just the signal the candidate needs to reach a key voting bloc.

Nowadays, celebrities share political panels and campaign stages with candidates regularly. The lines have been blurred. Americans have grown so accustomed to the nexus between Hollywood and politics that they are electing many familiar faces—singer Sonny Bono and *Love Boat* purser Fred Grandy became congressmen, action hero Arnold Schwarzenegger became a two-term governor, and actor Ronald Reagan became a two-term president. How did they do it? When asked by a group of students which experiences best prepared him for the presidency, Reagan once said, "You'd be surprised how much being a good actor pays off."

U.S. Capitol, Washington, D.C., August 1947. Aviator and millionaire film producer Howard Hughes prepares to testify before Congress. Hughes became embroiled in a political circus when Sen. Owen Brewster (R-ME) investigated Hughes's failure to deliver his "Spruce Goose" troop transport aircraft, calling it a "lumber yard that would never fly." Hughes took to the controls of the Spruce Goose and, before the eyes of the world, dramatically flew the "flying boat" before throngs of press. Brewster's committee never re-grouped. Hughes poured unlimited personal funds into the next Maine election, ensuring the end of Brewster's political career once and for all. (Courtesy U.S. Senate Historical Office.)

G8 Summit, Gleneagles, Scotland, July 2005. Pres. George W. Bush, rock star Bono, First Lady Laura Bush, and musician Bob Geldof hold a working meeting on Africa at the G8 Summit. Geldof praised Bush for delivering billions to fight disease and poverty and blasted the U.S. media for ignoring the achievement. Geldof said Bush "has done more than any other President so far. This is the triumph of American policy." (White House photograph by Eric Draper.)

Oval Office, the White House, 1963. Pres. John F. Kennedy had a hand in picking actor Cliff Robertson to portray him in his biopic *PT 109*. After Kennedy's first choice, Warren Beatty, thought the script was weak, Robertson found out Kennedy chose him for the role. When the movie was released, Kennedy admitted Beatty was right—the film was no good. It was a critical and box office flop. (Courtesy Cecil Stoughton, White House/John F. Kennedy Presidential Library, Boston.)

OVAL OFFICE, THE WHITE HOUSE, DECEMBER 1970. Superstar Elvis Presley poses for an official photograph with Pres. Richard M. Nixon. The photograph remains one of the most requested documents from the National Archives. Presley wrote Nixon a lengthy letter expressing disdain for hippie drug culture and asking to be named a "Federal Agent At Large." Nixon, eager to gain inroads with young people, granted Presley's wish and presented a badge from the U.S. Bureau of Narcotics and Dangerous Drugs. At Presley's request, the meeting remained a secret until the *Washington Post* broke the story in 1972. (Courtesy National Archives.)

ANOTHER VIEW OF THE OVAL OFFICE, THE WHITE HOUSE, DECEMBER 1970. Elvis Presley shows President Nixon cufflinks that had been given to him by Vice Pres. Spiro Agnew as Nixon aide Bud Krogh looks on. Presley also brought 8-by-10 photographs of his daughter (on the president's desk). White House staff hastily arranged the meeting when the singer stunned a guard at the West Gate by rolling up in a stretch limousine and asking to meet Nixon. Two hours later, "The King" was on his way into the Oval Office. (Courtesy National Archives.)

A THIRD VIEW OF THE OVAL OFFICE, THE WHITE HOUSE, DECEMBER 1970. Elvis invites members of his entourage into the Oval Office to meet the president. (Courtesy National Archives.)

Century Plaza Hotel, Los Angeles, California, June 1967. Comedian Jack Benny entertains Hollywood's elite assembled for Pres. Lyndon Johnson. The fund-raiser was a success inside the swank confines of the hotel, but outside, tens of thousands were protesting the Vietnam War. The protests turned violent as the crowd was beaten back by police. Though Benny and his Hollywood friends tried to boost Johnson's campaign, national divisiveness was too great. Johnson ultimately would not accept his party's nomination for another term. (Photograph by Yoichi R. Okamoto; courtesy LBJ Library.)

State Dining Room, the White House, June 1977. Avant-garde artist Andy Warhol presents Pres. Jimmy Carter with a portrait. After Watergate, the country wanted a Washington outsider. Endorsing the Warhol "campaign art" sent a clear signal that Carter was a progressive. The screen prints were sold to raise campaign cash. Carter credited the Warhol paintings as "one of the turning points in the financing of our campaign." (Courtesy Jimmy Carter Library.)

Reunion Arena, Dallas, Texas, August 1984. The once and future governors Pres. Ronald Reagan and blockbuster star Arnold Schwarzenegger are pictured at the Republican National Convention. Twenty years later, Schwarzenegger's political ambitions would be realized, becoming California's 38th governor—and its second actor-turned-governor. In 1967, actor Ronald Reagan became California's 33rd governor. (Courtesy Ronald Reagan Library.)

FAMILY MOVIE THEATER, THE WHITE HOUSE, JANUARY 1998. Pres. Bill Clinton, First Lady Hillary Clinton, and friends listen to actor/director Robert Duvall at a screening of his film *The Apostle*. In 1998, Clinton was embroiled in a scandal, having admitted to a sexual relationship with a White House intern. *The Apostle* was a film about sin and redemption in the Deep South—very near places Clinton spent most of his life. Afterward, Duvall told *Entertainment Weekly*, "Clinton said, 'This touched me.'" (Courtesy William J. Clinton Presidential Library.)

CENTURY PLAZA HOTEL, LOS ANGELES, CALIFORNIA, JUNE 1967. Hollywood mogul Lew Wasserman and Pres. Lyndon B. Johnson are shown at the President's Club Dinner. Wasserman was one of the most powerful men in Hollywood and perhaps its first lobbyist. In 1966, he installed Johnson confidante Jack Valenti as head of the Motion Picture Association of America. His influence grew so great that both Johnson and Jimmy Carter offered Wasserman cabinet positions. (Photograph by Yoichi R. Okamoto; courtesy LBJ Library.)

SENATE DINING ROOM, WASHINGTON, D.C., 1970S. Actor Marlon Brando dines with Sen. Charles Percy (R-IL). Brando wrote in *Songs My Mother Taught Me*, "Simply because you're a movie star, people empower you with special rights and privileges." Brando grew to understand those privileges, using his influence to stump for civil rights, better treatment for Native Americans, and fair housing. (Courtesy U.S. Senate Historical Office.)

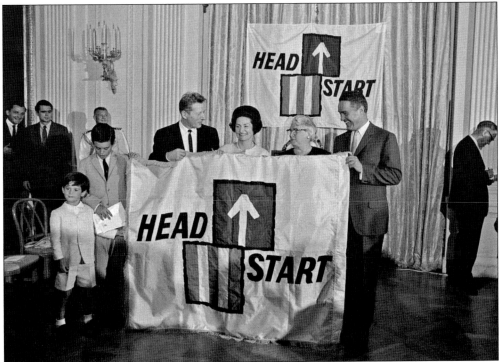

RED ROOM, THE WHITE HOUSE, WASHINGTON, D.C., JUNE 1965. Actor Danny Kaye (third from left) and Lady Bird Johnson kick off a ceremony for National Head Start Day. From left to right in the first row are Timothy Shriver, Robert Shriver, Kaye, Lady Bird, Mrs. Lou Maginn, and poverty director Sargent Shriver. Head Start was a major initiative of Johnson's administration, and he was determined to make a big splash. Kaye entertained the crowd and, more importantly, the press. (Courtesy LBJ Library.)

U.S. Capitol, Washington, D.C., March 1945. Vice Pres. Harry Truman promotes War Bonds with, from left to right, Carter T. Barron, actress Lana Turner, Adm. William Halsey, and Sen. Alben Barkley (R-KY). During World War II, Turner joined entertainers like Judy Garland, Bing Crosby—even Bugs Bunny—asking Americans to buy bonds. It was orchestrated through special government agencies, marking an official alliance between Hollywood and Washington to bolster the war effort. (Courtesy National Archives.)

Vets Auditorium, Des Moines, Iowa, December 2007. Television mogul Oprah Winfrey was big on boosting Barack Obama's candidacy early in his tough primary elections. Winfrey gave her first-ever endorsement, stumping for Obama in critical primary states. On the eve of Obama's presidential inauguration, Winfrey moved her show to the Kennedy Center, billing it "the hottest ticket in Oprah show history." (Courtesy Joe Crimmings Photography.)

OVAL OFFICE, THE WHITE HOUSE, NOVEMBER 1963. Pres. John F. Kennedy discusses plans for a Democratic National Committee (DNC) fund-raiser with, from left to right, John Bailey, DNC chairman; composer Richard Adler; singer/actress Lena Horne; Margaret Price; Broadway star Carol Lawrence; and others. The topic was raising money for next year's campaign, but Kennedy did not know how little time he had left for such meetings—he was assassinated in Dallas, Texas, two days later. (Courtesy Abbie Rowe, White House/John F. Kennedy Presidential Library, Boston.)

ROSE GARDEN, THE WHITE HOUSE, JULY 1987. Pres. Ronald Reagan speaks at a Take Pride in America event with actors Clint Eastwood and Louis Gossett Jr., who were enlisted to be national spokesmen. The organization is a national volunteer service to protect public parks, recreation areas, and cultural resources. Who better to go after litterbugs than two cinematic tough guys? (Courtesy Ronald Reagan Presidential Library.)

U.S. Capitol, Washington, D.C., Early 1970s. Rocker Mick Jagger is pictured at a press conference with Sen. Jacob Javits (R-NY). The Rolling Stones were under scrutiny in the United States for a slew of legal worries, not to mention publicly speaking out against the Vietnam War. When their American tour was threatened in the midst of all the turmoil, the Stones had friends in high places—Javits ensured the tour would take place as planned. (Courtesy U.S. Senate Historical Office.)

Diplomatic Reception Room, the White House, May 1984. "King of Pop" Michael Jackson receives a humanitarian award for his television advertisements curbing teen drinking and driving from Pres. Ronald Reagan and First Lady Nancy Reagan. Future Supreme Court justice John Roberts, then a young lawyer in the Reagan White House, denied Jackson a bigger award. After repeated requests from Jackson's publicity machine, Roberts wrote a confidential memo to his boss: "The office of Presidential correspondence is not yet an adjunct of Michael Jackson's PR firm." (Courtesy Ronald Reagan Library.)

ANGELS STADIUM, ANAHEIM, CALIFORNIA, APRIL 1989. Pres. George H. W. Bush and singer Gene Autry enjoy a Los Angeles Angels game. Autry, the first singing cowboy of American cinema, had a big hit with *Rudolph the Red-Nosed Reindeer*. He also made a fortune in broadcasting and was an original owner of the California Angels baseball team. He was a Bush family friend and lent plenty of financial support to Bush's campaign. (Courtesy George Bush Presidential Library.)

U.S. AMBASSADOR'S RESIDENCE, ACCRA, GHANA, FEBRUARY 2008. Pres. George W. Bush and First Lady Laura Bush congratulate singer Jordin Sparks, who sang the national anthem during a welcoming ceremony. Sparks, winner of the popular television show *American Idol*, traveled with the Bushes to the West African republic in an effort to draw attention to helping victims of malaria. (White House photograph by Eric Draper.)

MOTORCADE, FOUNTAIN VALLEY, CALIFORNIA, OCTOBER 1976. Pres. Gerald Ford campaigns for reelection with screen icon John Wayne. To stir up the crowd and add a little star power, Ford asked Wayne to introduce him at campaign events. Wayne's image as a lone cowboy riding the plains was appropriate to voters who were fatigued with Washington politicians after Watergate. But even the Wayne mystique could not save Ford, who lost to Jimmy Carter. (Courtesy Gerald R. Ford Library.)

OUTSIDE THE OVAL OFFICE, THE WHITE HOUSE, JULY 1962. During the cold war, artists could go places political leaders simply could not. President Kennedy had called upon famed clarinetist Benny Goodman to lead a cultural delegation to perform in the Soviet Union. Officials in Washington were eager for a full debrief of his trip upon return, as the Cuban Missile Crisis loomed over the nation with talk of nuclear war. (Robert Knudsen, White House/John F. Kennedy Presidential Library, Boston.)

Abou Ben Adhem Shrine Mosque, Springfield, Missouri, June 1952. Actor Ronald Reagan entertains Pres. Harry S. Truman, Gen. Harry Vaughan (left), and Mary Jane Truman (third from left); others are not identified. Reagan happened to be premiering his film *The Winning Team* when he heard Truman was in town for a World War I reunion. Reagan, a staunch Democrat at the time, jumped at the opportunity to perform for the president. (Courtesy Harry S. Truman Library.)

```
TELEGRAM                    MARCH 11, 1960

BY PHONE:  7:15 p.m.


MR. NAT COLE
401 SO. MUIRFIELD DRIVE
LOS ANGELES, CALIF.


I CERTAINLY APPRECIATE YOUR WILLINGNESS TO HELP ME IN THE

CAMPAIGN HERE IN WISCONSIN.  I WOULD LIKE TO HAVE HAD YOU

WITH ME ON MY VISITS AROUND THE STATE BUT I UNDERSTAND THAT

OUR SCHEDULES PRECLUDE US BEING HERE TOGETHER.  UNDER THESE

CIRCUMSTANCES I WOULD HOPE THAT IN ONE OF THE PRIMARIES THAT

IS TO FOLLOW WISCONSIN THAT YOU WOULD BE WILLING TO ASSIST

ME.  I AM MOST GRATEFUL TO YOU.  BEST REGARDS.


                        JOHN F. KENNEDY




CHARGED TO

ROBERT F. KENNEDY
SCHROEDER HOTEL
ROOM 1624
MILWAUKEE, WIS.
```

TELEGRAM, WISCONSIN TO CALIFORNIA, MARCH 1960. Presidential hopeful John F. Kennedy sent this telegram to popular singer Nat King Cole during the 1960 primaries. Cole was a principled African American entertainer selling records to largely white audiences in pre–civil rights America. Kennedy asked his help campaigning in key states. After Kennedy's Election Day victory, the trailblazing singer became a frequent consultant on civil rights to President Kennedy and later Pres. Lyndon Johnson. (Courtesy John F. Kennedy Presidential Library, Boston.)

DONOVAN HOTEL, WASHINGTON, D.C., JANUARY 2009. Actors Tim Robbins (left) and Josh Lucas attend the Creative Coalition's inaugural VIP dinner for Pres. Barack Obama. Both actors campaigned heavily for Obama; Lucas even knocked on college dorm room doors urging surprised coeds to vote. As for Robbins, he said he "couldn't sanction another Clinton in the White House," referring to Obama's Democratic opponent, Hillary Clinton. (Courtesy the Creative Coalition.)

SOUTH LAWN, THE WHITE HOUSE, MAY 1990. Pres. George H. W. Bush and First Lady Barbara Bush kick off the "Great American Workout Month" with Arnold Schwarzenegger and Sec. Louis Sullivan. Bush called Schwarzenegger "Conan the Republican" as a goof on his film *Conan the Barbarian.* Bush appointed him to lead the President's Council on Physical Fitness and Sports, giving Schwarzenegger political cachet. The action hero's future career in politics was taking shape. (Courtesy George Bush Presidential Library.)

FAMILY MOVIE THEATER, THE WHITE HOUSE, DECEMBER 1999. Pres. Bill Clinton greets Denzel Washington and boxer Rubin "Hurricane" Carter at a private screening of *The Hurricane*. The film told the story of the controversial imprisonment of a rising boxing star turned accused murderer. Clinton invited "Hurricane" Carter to the screening to honor him, despite lingering questions about Carter's innocence. But Clinton's mind was made up. *The Hollywood Reporter* wrote "a teary-eyed Pres. Clinton got up after the credits and announced, 'Mr. Carter, it's an honor to have you in this house.' " (Courtesy William J. Clinton Presidential Library.)

OVAL OFFICE, THE WHITE HOUSE, JANUARY 1983. Pres. Ronald Reagan "punches" boxing icon Muhammad Ali. Reagan's relationship with Ali was not always fun and games. In the late 1960s, Ali publicly refused the Vietnam draft. Then-governor Reagan vowed, "That draft dodger will never fight in my state, period." But bygones were bygones, and after Jesse Jackson dropped out, Ali supported Reagan during his 1984 campaign. (Courtesy Ronald Reagan Library.)

FAMILY MOVIE THEATER, THE WHITE HOUSE, MAY 1990. Martial arts actor Chuck Norris screens his new film *Delta Force 2* for Pres. George H. W. Bush and First Lady Barbara Bush. The actor, who publicly endorsed and campaigned for Bush, received Bush's help to start Kickstart, a nonprofit group that funds martial arts classes in local schools. For the record, Bush gave Norris's heroic drug-war film a "thumbs up." (Courtesy George Bush Presidential Library.)

SMITHSONIAN INSTITUTE, WASHINGTON, D.C., FEBRUARY 2007. Actor Will Smith poses with Motion Picture Association of America president Dan Glickman and Rep. Charlie Rangel (D-NY) at a film industry symposium against movie piracy. Though he had starred in several Hollywood blockbusters, some in Washington mistook the charismatic star for then-candidate Barack Obama, shouting, "We're going to vote for you, we love you Barack!" (Courtesy Motion Picture Association of America.)

SOUTH CAROLINA STATE UNIVERSITY, ORANGEBURG, SOUTH CAROLINA, JANUARY 2008. From left to right, R&B star Usher, actress Kerry Washington, presidential hopeful Barack Obama, South Carolina state representative Bakari Sellers, and comedian Chris Tucker are on stage during election 2008. Many of Obama's campaign events blended elements of political rally and rock concert. Young girls blew kisses to Usher and screamed for Tucker. As the candidate took the stage, there was frenzy in the crowd to see the departing stars. Obama grinned, saying "I'm going to wait. . . . They might cause a riot." (Courtesy Joe Crimmings Photography.)

CABINET ROOM, THE WHITE HOUSE, JUNE 1981. Pres. Ronald Reagan appointed actor Charlton Heston to a presidential task force to overview federal arts funding. As fellow conservatives, Reagan was sure Heston would conclude the National Endowment for the Arts was a needless expense. To Reagan's surprise, Heston concluded the funding was vital. (Courtesy Ronald Reagan Library.)

OVAL OFFICE, THE WHITE HOUSE, AUGUST 1982. Pres. Ronald Reagan (6 feet, 1 inch) looks up at Georgetown University basketball player Patrick Ewing (7 feet) as Sen. Robert Dole (6 feet, 1 inch) cracks a smile. Many sports stars get ceremonial visits to the White House, but this was official business. Even though Ewing was riding high from making it to the NCAA championship, he spent the summer working as a summer congressional page in Dole's office on Capitol Hill. (Courtesy Ronald Reagan Library.)

HARPO STUDIOS, CHICAGO, ILLINOIS, OCTOBER 1989. First Lady Barbara Bush promotes literacy on *The Oprah Winfrey Show*. For first ladies, life can resemble one nonstop whirlwind publicity tour. In her memoirs, Bush wrote, "I soon got used to waking up in hotel rooms and sleeping in strange beds." Oprah Winfrey, never shy to publicity, was increasingly featuring political guests on her popular show. (Courtesy George Bush Presidential Library.)

U.S. GOVERNMENT PUBLICITY STILL, 1942. Movie star Rita Hayworth asks Americans to sacrifice car bumpers for a World War II scrap metal campaign. Even Hayworth's 1941 Lincoln Continental has a sacrificial bumper propped up on the left. Metal was needed for everything from guns and grenades to ships and fighter planes, and publicity campaigns like this demonstrated the two-front war America was fighting—overseas and on the home front. (Courtesy National Archives.)

U.S. CAPITOL, WASHINGTON, D.C. Hayworth visits Washington in a flurry of wartime publicity. She joined the ranks of Betty Grable and Lana Turner as not only the most popular pinup girl for lonely servicemen overseas, but also a tireless spokeswoman for wartime programs. (Courtesy National Archives.)

INTERNET ADVERTISEMENT, FEBRUARY 2008. Actor Jack Nicholson supports Democratic presidential hopeful Hillary Rodham Clinton appearing in an Internet advertisement. Calling Clinton "the best man for the job," Nicholson added his name to an increasing number of celebrities taking to the Internet to endorse political candidates. The advertisement, titled "Jack and Hill," was an overnight sensation generating millions of Internet hits. The rascally actor even signed off, "I'm Jack Nicholson and I approve this message." Responding to criticism of celebrities sticking their nose in politics, he told *MTV News*, "I wish they'd stop calling us 'Hollywood nitwits.' They can't get along without us. We've got our share of nitwits. I've been called a 'woolly headed intellectual,' neither of which is accurate. I only wish I was woolly headed." (Courtesy Foundation for a Better Tomorrow.)

ACROSS AMERICA, PEOPLE ARE DISCOVERING
SOMETHING WONDERFUL. THEIR HERITAGE.

Arcadia Publishing is the leading local history publisher in the United States. With more than 5,000 titles in print and hundreds of new titles released every year, Arcadia has extensive specialized experience chronicling the history of communities and celebrating America's hidden stories, bringing to life the people, places, and events from the past. To discover the history of other communities across the nation, please visit:

www.arcadiapublishing.com

Customized search tools allow you to find regional history books about the town where you grew up, the cities where your friends and family live, the town where your parents met, or even that retirement spot you've been dreaming about.